THE

REFERENCE

SHELF

AFFIRMATIVE ACTION

edited by ROBERT EMMET LONG

THE REFERENCE SHELF

Volume 68 Number 3

THE H. W. WILSON COMPANY

New York   Dublin   1996

THE REFERENCE SHELF

The books in this series contain reprints of articles, excerpts from books, addresses on current issues, and studies of social trends in the United States and other countries. There are six numbers to a volume, all of which are usually published in a single calendar year. Numbers one through five devote themselves to a single subject, give background information and discussion from various points of view, concluding with a comprehensive bibliography that contains books, pamphlets, and abstracts of additional articles on the subject. The final number is a collection of recent speeches. This number also contains a subject index to the entire Reference Shelf volume. Books in the series may be purchased individually or on subscription.

Library of Congress Cataloging-in-Publication Data

Main entry under title:

Affirmative action / edited by Robert Emmet Long.
     p. cm. — (The Reference shelf ; v. 68, no. 3)
    Includes bibliographical references.
    ISBN 0-8242-0888-9
    1. Affirmative action programs—United States.   I. Long, Robert
Emmet. II. Series.
HF5549.5.A34A42   1996
331.13'3'0973—dc20   96-16236
                                         CIP

Cover: A group demonstrates in front of the White House. *Photo*: Bettmann

Printed in the United States of America

CONTENTS

IV. THE NATIONAL DEBATE

Within the last few years the social policy known as affirmative action has emerged as a key political issue on the national scene, one that is likely to play a prominent role in the presidential election in 1996. Affirmative action came into being during the fervent years of Lyndon Johnson's *Great Society*. Passage of the Civil Rights Act of 1964 gave birth to it, together with its commission, the Equal Employment Opportunity Commission (EEOC), which at first had little power but whose authority grew steadily. During the 1960s the EEOC was imbued with a kind of missionary zeal in correcting previous wrongs to blacks. In college admissions and employment, blacks—later other disadvantaged ethnic groups and women—were given a chance to catch up, to find their place on a level playing field with white male breadwinners. Early on, there were cries of "reverse discrimination," but they went largely unheeded; the momentum of the period favored the liberal activists.

By the 1980s, however, with Presidents Reagan and Bush in the White House, a more conservative mood had come over the country, and affirmative action began to be questioned and disputed. Still, neither Reagan nor Bush, although speaking against affirmative action, made any move to strike it down and in fact were quiet practitioners of it in their administrative appointments. It was the emergence to power of the Republican party's right wing in the congressional election of 1994 that changed everything. What had been measured dissent now became a vehement demand that affirmative action be abolished. This is the situation that exists today, with a debate in progress and the bandying of catch words like "colorblind society" and "meritocracy." This compilation of articles attempts to document the debate and to sketch its dimensions.

Section One begins with articles that sketch out the controversial history of affirmative action since its inception a generation ago. The articles reveal that affirmative action was intended to lend assistance to blacks and did not apply to other ethnic groups or to women. The enlarged powers of the EEOC and the expanded coverage of individuals coming under its protection occurred with a kind of snowballing effect. College admission quotas were mandated, as were quotas for hiring by the federal government and by companies doing business with it; a certain number of contracts was also "set aside" for minority-owned firms doing business with the government. In 1978, however, the Supreme Court ruled in the *Bakke* case that quotas in college and graduate school admissions were unacceptable, though the disadvantaged status of an applicant could be taken into account. The vagueness of this ruling did not decisively alter the status of affirmative action, but it did begin a process of steady erosion and today affirmative action is under threat of being abolished. Several other articles focus upon the California Civil Rights Initiative, which, if passed, would bar any form of affirmative action preference—whether involving race, gender, ethnicity, or national origin—in state hiring, contracting, and education.

Section Two is concerned with pending legislation and court cases that will affect the future of affirmative action. In Congress the Republican right wing is now mounting an assault on affirmative action, which may place President Clinton in an extremely difficult position. For if he comes out strongly for affirmative action he stands to lose the endorsement of disaffected white males, but if he retreats on the issue he will lose the support of his black constituency. Affirmative action thus becomes a "wedge issue" that Republicans hope will divide the Democrats and gravely weaken them in the 1996 election. Recent decisions in the courts, meanwhile, show a steady chipping away at affirmative action programs.

Section Three deals with college admissions and job hirings, where quotas are a paramount issue. An opening article discusses the dilemma of the admissions program at UCLA, which has many African- and Mexican-American applicants but relatively few who can meet its admissions standards. Attempting to be fair to all concerned, the university created a two-tier system in which 60 percent of the students (predominately white and Asian-American) were selected on the basis of their superior test scores. A second group (made up largely of African- and Mexican-Americans) were selected for admission on a basis that takes racial and family disadvantages into account. The procedure may be a tricky shuffle, but without it minorities would make up only a small fraction of the student body. Another article, on affirmative action and the work force, focuses on Chicago. The police department has attempted to satisfy both blacks and whites in its promotions, but with mixed results. At first a quota system was tried, which angered whites; then promotions were awarded according to those with the highest test scores, which angered blacks. The present arrangement, which makes no one perfectly happy but leaves no one feeling enraged, is a blend of both approaches. Affirmative action, thus far, has worked best in Chicago's business community, where some companies, such as Allstate, have model affirmative action programs. Even if affirmative action were to be terminated tomorrow, companies would still be likely to appreciate the benefits of diversity in the workforce. Other articles take up the issue, pro and con, of set-asides for minority contractors, a program that works sometimes, but has also been abused.

The debate over affirmative action is elaborated more fully in Section Four. This section opens with articles by two conservatives, who argue that affirmative action has produced few results: the condition of blacks is approximately what it would have been had affirmative action not existed. Their argument is countered by two liberal writers who contend that affirmative action has, in fact, benefitted blacks who otherwise would face far greater discrimination and exclusion. Two other articles explore the notion of a meritocracy.

The editor is indebted to the authors and publishers who have granted permission to reprint the materials in this collection. Special thanks are due to the staff of Penfield Library, State University of New York College at Oswego.

ROBERT EMMET LONG

February 1996

I. THE CALIFORNIA CIVIL RIGHTS INITIATIVE

Editor's Introduction

The articles in this section deal with the background of affirmative action from its inception thirty years ago to its threatened termination in the l990s. The lead article, by Tony Mauro writing in *USA Today*, traces affirmative action's origins to Lyndon Johnson's inauguration of the *Great Society*, and the passage of the Civil Rights Act of 1964, which prohibited discrimination in public education and employment. The Civil Rights Act also established the Equal Employment Opportunity Commission (EEOC), which monitors and enforces compliance with the Act's provisions. This legislation was later expanded in the 1972 Equal Employment Opportunity Act to include all companies with more than fifteen employees. But Mauro comments, too, on affirmative action in the courts, and the failure of the policy to create any significant upward mobility for blacks.

In a related piece reprinted from *Commentary*, Arch Puddington discusses the evolution of affirmative action into what perversion of its original intention. Originally, it was enacted to apply to blacks only, to redress intentional discrimination. It was to be strictly understood, moreover, that no quotas in hiring or in other practices were to be permitted. Yet following the passage of this legislation, not only blacks but also women and other minorities began to receive affirmative action preference. The EEOC mandated quotas ranging from college admissions to hiring of public employees and the awarding of federal contracts. Puddington argues for an elimination of all federal programs that extend preference on the basis of race (as well as ethnicity or gender), but would keep in place other safeguards against discrimination.

Several articles then follow on the referendum on affirmative action in California that will influence the fate of the program not only on the West Coast but also across the nation. In an article in *Newsweek*, Howard Fineman discusses the implications of the California Civil Rights Initiative (CCRI), which would bar any form of affirmative action preference in state hiring, contracting, or education. CCRI has become a key "wedge issue" advanced by

11

the Republican opposition to divide the Democrats in the 1996 presidential election. John H. Bunzel, in an address in *Vital Speeches of the Day*, is sympathetic to the California initiative but wary of its absoluteness, which makes no provision for diversity in college admissions and job hirings. Nicolaus Mills, in an article in *Dissent*, reflects on the strong likelihood that the CCRI, supported according to a *Los Angeles Times* poll by 73 percent of Californians, will become law. Its passage would undoubtedly put the Democrats at bay, but might well raise against the Republicans the accusation of a meanness of spirit in managing ethnic relations.

MORE THAN EQUAL OPPORTUNITY, LESS THAN QUOTAS[1]

In an angry, handwritten memo, the nation's first black Supreme Court justice told his white colleagues why America needed *affirmative* action.

"We are not yet all equals," Thurgood Marshall wrote in a 1978 note that recently came to light. "As to this country being a melting pot—either the Negro did not get in the pot or he did not get melted down." The Court went on that year, in the landmark *Bakke* case, to strike down a racial quota that kept a white male out of a California medical school. But it said using the race of applicants as a "plus factor" in a less formal way—without strict quotas—was acceptable.

Ever since then, affirmative action has been attacked, praised, and misunderstood—but also largely accepted in the American workplace. It has been endorsed by political leaders from Richard Nixon and Robert Dole to Jesse Jackson, and embraced by many corporations and government agencies, large and small. But what is it? And why has it risen to the top of the political and legal agenda? Lack of definition.

The term affirmative action encompasses a range of measures aimed at compensating for past discrimination by increasing the

[1]Article by Tony Mauro, staff writer, from *USA Today* Mr 24 '95. Copyright © 1995 by *USA TODAY*. Reprinted with permission.

chances that minorities or women will be chosen for jobs, promotions, admissions, or contracts. It's more than equal opportunity—encouraging minorities and women to apply for jobs, promotions, or contracts. But it is less than quotas, whereby jobs don't get filled until a minority is found.

Within that spectrum, a definition of what is legal and what is not legal has shifted, sometimes depending on what kind of employer is involved. In fact, some forms of affirmative action seem to be banned outright in the main federal law on the subject. The 1964 Civil Rights Act prohibits workplace discrimination on the basis of "race, color, religion, sex, or national origin." That law also says it should not be interpreted to require any employer "to grant preferential treatment to any individual or to any group."

It wasn't long before it became clear to many that passing a law simply banning bias was not enough. In 1965, Lyndon Johnson signed an executive order telling companies that receive federal funds to establish minority hiring goals—but not quotas. "Some people were simply not going to change unless you ordered them, 'The next person you hire is black,'" says University of Washington law professor Eric Schnapper, a longtime civil rights lawyer.

The so-called Philadelphia plan, instituted under Nixon in 1969, required federal contractors to set goals for minority hiring. The number of minorities in construction jobs jumped from 1 percent to 12 percent. Unions and employers protested at first, but learned to live with affirmative action plans—some of which might not pass legal muster today. "It was the lesser of two evils," recalls Washington lawyer David Copus, a former government official who helped force AT&T to hire more minorities in the early 1970s. "Better to do this than be accused of violating the law."

The Backlash

But as the years have passed, more and more uneasiness has built up among white males and others toward programs that clearly give preference on the basis of race. "Twenty years ago, most white people had pretty direct knowledge of what was going on with black people," says Schnapper. "Now, the only race-conscious thing that young people see may be affirmative action. Bull Connor isn't on TV anymore."

The Court's Role

The Supreme Court, once the key champion of affirmative action, has also shifted. Marshall, who fought for affirmative action, was replaced in 1991 by Clarence Thomas, who says it stigmatizes blacks and holds them back. Some basic principles gleaned from court rulings on affirmative action: It's remedial. The Court has said there ought to be some evidence of past bias as a backdrop for whatever boost, bonus or remedy that is being given to minorities or women today.

In 1989, justices struck down a Richmond, VA, plan that required 30 percent of city subcontracts to go to minority-owned companies. Not enough evidence of past bias, the Court said. Related issues—such as how recent the past bias has to be—are much less clear. It can't dislodge whites. The courts have generally looked kindly toward plans that boost minorities' chances of getting hired—even though some pool of white applicants did not get the job. Those whites, in theory, have other doors to knock on. But plans that called for laying off or firing specific whites to make room for blacks have generally been struck down.

"There is a fundamental difference between not being hired and being fired," says Darien McWhirter, author of *Your Rights at Work*. "Affirmative action that causes you to fire white people is illegal." A New Jersey case on its way to the Supreme Court may test that rule. The Clinton administration has sided with the Piscataway school system, which used race as a "tie-breaker" when it chose to lay off a white teacher and retain a black teacher with roughly equal seniority. It can't exclude all whites. "If the sign goes up, 'Whites need not apply,' it won't fly," says Copus, who advises employers on affirmative action. That principle is what led the Court to agree with Allan Bakke in 1978 and strike down the University of California-Davis program excluding whites from 16 of 100 medical school openings.

[In February 1995] . . . the Justice Department sued Illinois State University, challenging a training program that considered only those applications from minorities or females. "When individuals are absolutely precluded from getting a job because of their gender or race, we have an obligation to enforce the law," says Assistant Attorney General Deval Patrick.

An affirmative action plan should have an end. In 1979 and 1986, the Court approved two plans—one for steelworkers, one for firefighters—that set goals for minority hiring that had an end.

Justice Harry Blackmun wrote in the *Bakke* case that "in order to get beyond racism, we must first take account of race." He hoped for the time "when an 'affirmative action' program is . . . a relic of the past," and guessed that would take about ten years. Seventeen years later, the courts, Congress and society are looking at whether the time has come to turn affirmative action into a relic.

WHAT TO DO ABOUT AFFIRMATIVE ACTION[2]

The thinking behind the policy of racial preference which has been followed in America over the past quarter-century under the name of "affirmative action" is best summed up by former Supreme Court Justice Harry Blackmun's famous dictum that, "In order to get beyond racism, we must first take race into account."

The Orwellian quality of Blackmun's admonition is obvious. Seldom has a democratic government's policy so completely contradicted the core values of its citizenry as racial preference does in violating the universally held American ideals of fairness and individual rights, including the right to be free from discrimination. Not surprisingly, then, where Americans regarded the original civil-rights legislation as representing a long-overdue fulfillment of the country's democratic promise, they overwhelmingly see racial preference as an undemocratic and alien concept, a policy implemented by stealth and subterfuge and defended by duplicity and legalistic tricks.

Americans do not believe that past discrimination against blacks in the workplace justifies present discrimination against whites. Nor do they accept the thesis that tests and standards are tainted, *en masse*, by cultural bias against minorities. Having been taught in high-school civics classes that gerrymandering to ensure party domination represents a defect in democracy, Americans

[2]Article by Arch Puddington, a senior scholar at Freedom House, from *Commentary* 99:21–8 Je '95. Copyright © 1995 by *Commentary*. Reprinted with permission. All rights reserved.

are bewildered by the argument that gerrymandering is necessary to ensure the political representation of blacks and Hispanics. They are unimpressed by the contention that a university's
excellence is enhanced by the mere fact of racial and ethnic diversity in its student body, especially when entrance requirements
must be lowered substantially to achieve that goal.

Americans, in short, oppose racial preference in all its embod-
iments, and have signified their opposition in opinion poll after
opinion poll, usually by margins of three to one or more, with
women as strongly opposed as men, and with an impressive proportion of blacks indicating opposition as well. The contention,
repeatedly advanced by advocates of preferential policies, that a
national consensus exists in support of such policies has been true
only at the level of political elites. Americans do support what
might be called soft affirmative action, entailing special recruitment, training, and outreach efforts, and are willing to accept
some short-term compensatory measures to rectify obvious cases
of proven discrimination. But attitudes have, if anything, har-
dened against the kind of aggressive, numbers-driven preference
schemes increasingly encountered in university admissions and
civil-service hiring.

Nonetheless . . . racial preference in its various manifesta-
tions has been impressively resistant to calls for reform, much less
elimination. In fact, race consciousness has begun to insinuate itself into areas which, common sense alone would suggest, should
be immune to intrusive government social engineering. To cite
but one example of this disturbing trend: Congress has mandated
that guidelines be established guaranteeing the involvement of
minorities (and women) in clinical research—a form of scientific
experimentation by quota.

There is, furthermore, reason to question whether the advocates of race-conscious social policy continue to take seriously the
objective of getting "beyond race," a condition which presumably
would warrant the elimination of all preferential programs. The
late Thurgood Marshall, an outspoken champion of preference
while on the Supreme Court, is reported to have blurted out during an in-chambers discussion that blacks would need affirmative
action for a hundred years. A similar opinion has been expressed
by Benjamin Hooks, the former director of the National Association for the Advancement of Colored People (NAACP). Hooks

contends that affirmative action in some form should be accepted as one of those permanent, irritating features of American life— he cited as examples speeding laws and the April 15 income-tax deadline—which citizens tolerate as essential to the efficient and just functioning of society.

Neither Marshall nor Hooks is regarded as an extremist on race matters; their advocacy of a permanent regime of affirmative action falls within the mainstream of present-day liberal thought. The promotion of "diversity"—the latest euphemism for preferential representation—is as fundamental to liberal governance as was the protection of labor unions in an earlier era. And until very recently, liberal proponents of preference clearly believed that history was on their side.

Thus, where enforcement agencies were formerly cautious in pressing affirmative action on the medical profession, the Clinton administration was formulating plans for a quota system throughout the health-care workforce. The goal, according to one memo of Hillary Clinton's task force, was nothing less than to ensure that this workforce achieve "sufficient racial, ethnic, gender, geographic, and cultural diversity to be representative of the people it serves." The task force also had plans to guide minority doctors into specialties while tracking other doctors into general practice. To realize this medical-care diversity blueprint, the task force proposed the creation of a bureaucracy with coercive powers to regulate the "geographic" and "cultural" distribution of physicians and other medical practitioners.

How did America drift from the ideal of a color-blind society to the current environment of quotas, goals, timetables, race-norming, set-asides, diversity-training, and the like?

Those troubled by this question often refer wistfully to Martin Luther King, Jr.'s declaration that he hoped to see the day when his children would be judged by the content of their character and not by the color of their skin. Yet it must be recognized that even when King uttered those inspirational words at the 1963 March on Washington, they no longer reflected the thinking of crucial segments of the civil-rights movement. Already, increasingly influential black activists and their white supporters were advancing demands for hiring plans based on racial quotas. In pressing for such plans (then called compensatory treatment), the civil-rights movement was being joined by officials from the

Kennedy administration, as well as by white intellectuals who, going further, announced that black economic equality could never be attained without a wholesale adjustment of standards and the merit principle.

These ruminations were not lost on the Dixiecrat opponents of desegregation, and the charge was soon made that Title VII of the pending civil-rights bill—the section dealing with discrimination in the workplace—would lead to the widespread practice of reverse discrimination. This in turn provoked a series of statements and speeches by stalwart liberals like Senators Hubert Humphrey, Joseph Clark, and Clifford Case, adamantly and unequivocally denying that the bill could be interpreted to permit racial preference.

In order to dispel lingering doubts, Humphrey and other supporters inserted an amendment to the bill declaring flatly that the law's purpose was to rectify cases of intentional discrimination and that it was not intended to impose sanctions simply because a workplace contained few blacks or because few blacks passed an employment test. Armed with this and similar clauses prohibiting reverse discrimination, Humphrey promised to "start eating the pages [of the civil-rights bill] one after another" if anyone could discover language in it "which provides that an employer will have to hire on the basis of percentage or quota."

Under normal circumstances, the insertion of unambiguous anti-preference language, combined with the condemnations of reverse discrimination by the bill's sponsors, would have been sufficient to prevent the subsequent distortion of the law's intent. But these protections turned out to be useless against the determination of the country's elites (in the political system, in the media, in the universities, and in the courts) to override them. Having concluded (especially after the urban riots of the late 1960s) that social peace demanded racial preference, political leaders from both parties, along with a growing number of intellectuals and activists, both white and black, began looking upon the anti-preference clauses in Title VII as obstacles to be circumvented rather than guides to be followed. The anti-preference language which had been added to ensure passage of the Civil Rights Act of 1964 was now not only ignored but treated as though it did not even exist.

Hence there was no serious effort by either Congress or the courts or anyone else to rein in the civil-rights bureaucracy, which dismissed the anti-preference provisions with contempt from the very outset. A "big zero, a nothing, a nullity," is how these provisions were characterized by an official of the Equal Employment Opportunity Commission (EEOC) at the time. Federal enforcement officials in general, most of whom were white, were more aggressive in pursuing preferences, and less inclined to reflect on the broader implications of affirmative action, than were many mainstream black leaders of that day, some of whom—Roy Wilkins, Bayard Rustin, and Clarence Mitchell, for example—opposed reverse discrimination on moral and political grounds.

The part played by the EEOC in putting together the structure of racial preference cannot be overstated. In blithe and conscious disregard of the anti-preference sections of Title VII, EEOC officials broadened the definition of discrimination to encompass anything which contributed to unequal outcomes. In its most far-reaching move, the EEOC launched an all-out assault on employment testing. The agency's mindset was reflected in comments about "irrelevant and unreasonable standards," "the cult of credentialism," and "artificial barriers."

Yet despite the ingenuity of its lawyers in devising intricate arguments to circumvent the strictures against reverse discrimination—and despite the willingness of activist judges to accept these arguments—the EEOC could never have achieved its aims had it not been for a transformation of elite attitudes toward the problem of race in America.

In 1964, the year the Civil Rights Act was passed, an optimistic and morally confident America believed that the challenge posed by the "Negro revolution" could be met through a combination of anti-discrimination laws, economic growth, and the voluntary good will of corporations, universities, and other institutions. But by the decade's end, a crucial segment of elite opinion had concluded that America was deeply flawed, even sick, and that racism, conscious or otherwise, permeated every institution and government policy. Where individual prejudice had previously been identified as the chief obstacle to black progress, now a new target, "institutional racism," was seen as the principal villain. And where it was once thought that democratic guarantees against discrimination, plus the inherent fairness of the American people, were sufficient to overcome injustice, the idea now took hold that since racism was built into the social order, coercive measures were required to root it out.

In this view, moreover, the gradualist Great Society approach launched by Lyndon Johnson, which stressed education, training, and the strengthening of black institutions, could not alleviate the misery of the inner-city poor, at least not as effectively as forcing employers to hire them. Even Johnson himself began calling for affirmative action and issued an executive order directing that federal contractors adopt hiring policies which did not discriminate on the basis of race (or gender); in a process that would soon become all too familiar, court decisions and the guidelines of regulators subsequently interpreted the directive as mandating racial balance in the workforce, thus paving the way for demands that companies doing business with the government institute what often amounted to quotas in order to qualify for contracts.

Little noticed at the time—or, for that matter, later—was that black America was in the midst of a period of unprecedented economic progress, during which black poverty declined, the racial income gap substantially narrowed, black college enrollment mushroomed, and black advancement into the professions took a substantial leap forward. All this, it should be stressed, occurred *prior* to the introduction of government-mandated racial preference.

Once affirmative action got going, there was no holding it back. The civil-rights movement and those responsible for implementing civil-rights policy simply refused to accept an approach under which preference would be limited to cases of overt discrimination, or applied to a narrow group of crucial institutions, such as urban police departments, where racial integration served a pressing public need. Instead, every precedent was exploited to further the permanent entrenchment of race consciousness.

For example, the Philadelphia Plan, the first preferential policy to enjoy presidential backing (the President being Richard Nixon), was a relatively limited effort calling for racial quotas in the Philadelphia building trades, an industry with a notorious record of racial exclusion. Yet this limited program was seized upon by the EEOC and other agencies as a basis for demanding hiring-by-the-numbers schemes throughout the economy, whether or not prior discrimination could be proved.

Similarly, once a race-conscious doctrine was applied to one institution, it inevitably expanded its reach into other arenas. The Supreme Court's decision in *Griggs v. Duke Power, Inc.*—that employment tests could be found to constitute illegal discrimination if blacks failed at a higher rate than whites—was ostensibly confined to hiring and promotion. But *Griggs* was used to legitimize the burgeoning movement against testing and standards in the educational world as well. Tracking by intellectual ability, special classes for high achievers, selective high schools requiring admissions tests, standardized examinations for university admissions—all were accused of perpetuating historic patterns of bias.

The campaign against testing and merit in turn gave rise to a series of myths about the economy, the schools, the workplace, about America itself. Thus, lowering job standards as a means of hiring enough blacks to fill a quota was justified on the grounds that merit had never figured prominently in the American workplace, that the dominant principles had always been nepotism, back-scratching, and conformism. To explain the racial gap in Scholastic Aptitude Test (SAT) scores, the concept of cultural bias was advanced, according to which disparities in results derived from the tests' emphasis on events and ideas alien to urban black children. Another theory claimed that poor black children were not accustomed to speaking standard English and were therefore placed at a disadvantage in a normal classroom environment. It was duly proposed that black children be taught much like immigrant children, with bilingual classes in which both standard English and black English would be utilized. A related theory stated that black children retained a distinct learning style which differed in significant respects from the learning styles of other children. As one educator expressed the theory, any test which stressed "logical, analytical methods of problem-solving" would *ipso facto* be biased against blacks.

Until quite recently, the very idea of abolishing racial preference was unthinkable; the most realistic ambitions for the critics of race-based social policy went no further than trying to limit—limit, not stop—the apparently relentless spread of racial preferences throughout the economy, the schools and universities, and the political system. Yet it now appears not only that the momentum of racial preference has been halted, but that, at a minimum, a part of the imposing affirmative-action edifice will be dismantled. Furthermore, a process has already been set in motion which could conceivably lead to the virtual elimination of race-based programs.

Racial preferences have become vulnerable mainly because of the sudden collapse of the elite consensus which always sustained affirmative action in the face of popular opposition. Where in the past many Republicans could be counted on to support, or at least tolerate, racial preferences, the new congressional majority seems much more inclined to take a sharply critical look at existing racial policies. Equally important is the erosion of support for preference within the Democratic party. While some newly skeptical Democrats are clearly motivated by worries about reelection, others have welcomed the opportunity to express long-suppressed reservations about policies which they see as having corrupted, divided, and weakened their party.

The revolt against affirmative action has also been heavily influenced by the fact that, as preferential policies have extended throughout the economy, a critical mass of real or perceived victims of reverse discrimination has been reached—white males who have been denied jobs, rejected for promotion, or prevented from attending the college or professional school of their choice because slots were reserved for blacks (or other minorities or women).

There is, no doubt, an inclination on the part of white men to blame affirmative action when they are passed over for jobs or promotions, a tendency which is reinforced by the atmosphere of secrecy surrounding most preference programs. But enough is known about affirmative action in the public sector through information which has come out in the course of litigation to conclude that thousands of whites have indeed been passed over for civil-service jobs and university admissions because of outright quotas for racial minorities. It is also clear that a considerable number of private businesses have been denied government contracts because of minority set-asides.

Another major factor in the change of attitude toward affirmative action is the California Civil Rights Initiative (CCRI), which has already had an incalculable impact. The CCRI was organized by two white, male, and politically moderate professors in the California state-university system. The measure would amend the California constitution to prohibit the state government or any state agency (including the university system) from granting preference on the basis of race, ethnicity, or gender in employment, college admissions, or the awarding of contracts. It would, in other words, effectively ban affirmative-action programs mandated by the state.

Though limited to California, the CCRI is at heart a response to the logical destination of affirmative action everywhere in America: quota systems sustained by the support of elites from both political parties. To be sure, policy by racial classification has grown more pervasive in California than elsewhere in America. White males have been told not to bother applying for positions with the Los Angeles fire department due to the need to fill minority quotas. In San Francisco, Chinese students are denied admission to a selective public high school because of an ethnic cap; for similar reasons, whites, mainly Jews and East European immigrants, are often denied admission to magnet schools in Los Angeles. A de-facto quota system effectively denies white males the opportunity to compete for faculty positions at certain state colleges. And, incredibly enough, the state legislature passed a bill calling for ethnic "guidelines" not only for admission to the state-university system but for graduation as well. The bill was vetoed by Governor Pete Wilson; had a Democrat been governor, it would almost certainly have become law.

The true impact of the CCRI can be gauged by the degree of fear it has generated among supporters of affirmative action. So long as the debate could be limited to the courts, the agencies of race regulation, and, when unavoidable, the legislative arena, affirmative action was secure. The mere threat of taking the issue directly to the voters, as the CCRI's sponsors propose to do through the referendum process, has elicited a downright panicky response—itself a clear indication that the advocates of racial preference understand how unpopular their case is, and how weak.

But a note of caution must be sounded to those who believe that current developments will lead inexorably to the reinstitution of color-blindness as the reigning principle in racial matters. The resilience of affirmative action in the face of widespread popular hostility suggests that even a modest change of course could prove a difficult and highly divisive affair.

There is, to begin with, the fact that affirmative action has been introduced largely by skirting the normal democratic process of debate and legislative action. Affirmative action is by now rooted in literally thousands of presidential directives, court decisions, enforcement-agency guidelines, and regulatory rules. These will not easily be overturned.

There is also the complicating factor of the federal judiciary's central role in overseeing racial policy. Given the emotionally charged character of the racial debate, the critics of racial preference will be tempted to postpone legislative action in the hope that the Supreme Court will resolve the issue once and for all. But while the Court today is less prone to judicial activism than during the Warren and Burger years, and while it may decide to limit the conditions under which a preferential program can be applied, it is unlikely to do away with affirmative action altogether.

The Republicans will face another temptation: to exploit white hostility to racial preference but avoid serious political action to eliminate it. A powerful political logic lies behind this temptation, since getting rid of affirmative action would also deprive the Republicans of a potent wedge issue. Yet one can hardly imagine a less desirable outcome than a prolonged and angry political confrontation over race. Moreover, if responsible politicians who share a principled opposition to preference decline to take the initiative, the door will be opened to racists and unscrupulous demagogues.

An additional obstacle to change is the fact that eliminating affirmative action does not offer much of a financial payoff. Affirmative action is not expensive; its only direct cost to the taxpayer is the expense of maintaining civil-rights agencies like the EEOC.

Claims have been made that affirmative action does represent a major cost to the American economy, but the facts are unclear since neither the media nor scholarly researchers nor the corporations themselves have shown an interest in undertaking an investigation of its economic impact. Indeed, though affirmative action is one of the most intensely discussed social issues of the day, it is probably the least researched. Press coverage is generally limited to the political debate; seldom are stories done about the actual functioning of affirmative-action programs. Nor is there much serious scholarly investigation of such questions as affirmative action's impact on employee morale, the performance of students admitted to college on an affirmative-action track, or the degree to which contract set-asides have contributed to the establishment of stable minority businesses.

Given the truly massive amount of research devoted to racial issues over the years, the lack of attention to preferential policies raises the suspicion that what has been operating here is a deliberate decision to avoid knowing the details of affirmative action's inner workings out of fear of the public reaction.

Opponents of racial preference must also contend with the widespread acceptance of the "diversity" principle within certain key institutions. Here the American university stands out for its uncritical embrace of the notion that, as one recent cliché has it, "diversity is part of excellence." When Francis Lawrence, the president of Rutgers University, came under fire for uttering the now-famous phrase which seemed to question the genetic capabilities of black students, his principal defense—indeed practically his only defense—was that he had increased minority enrollment at Rutgers and during a previous administrative stint at Tulane. True to form, no one bothered to ask how black students recruited under Lawrence's diversity initiatives had fared academically or psychologically, or how the campus racial atmosphere had been affected, or how much standards had been adjusted to achieve the quota. The body count, and the body count alone, was what mattered for Lawrence, and, it would seem, for administrators at many campuses.

The diversity principle is also firmly entrenched throughout government service. Most agencies include a diversity or affirmative-action department, headed by an official with deputy-level status, with intrusive authority to promote staff "balance" and minority participation in contract bidding. So, too, private corporations have accepted affirmative action as part of the price of doing business. Large corporations, in fact, can usually be counted on to oppose anti-quota legislation, preferring the simplicity of hiring by the numbers to the uncertainty of more flexible systems and the increased possibilities of anti-discrimination litigation brought by minorities or by whites claiming reverse bias.

But of course the most serious obstacle to change is black America's strong attachment to affirmative action. Race-conscious policies have had no demonstrable effect at all on the black poor, but they are widely perceived as having played a crucial role in creating the first mass black middle class in American history. The claim here is wildly exaggerated—to repeat, the trend was already well advanced before affirmative action got going. Nevertheless, to many blacks, affirmative action has become not a series of temporary benefits but a basic civil right, almost as fundamental as the right to eat at a restaurant or live in the neighborhood of one's choice, and certainly more important than welfare.

Accordingly, black leaders, who are always quick to condemn even the most modest changes as "turning back the clock" or as a threat to the gains of the civil-rights movement, have now escalated the counterattack in response to the more sweeping recent challenge to affirmative action. When Governor Pete Wilson made some favorable comments about the CCRI, Jesse Jackson compared him to George Wallace blocking the schoolhouse door in Jim Crow Alabama. And when congressional Republicans moved to rescind a set-aside program in the communications industry, Representative Charles Rangel, a Democrat from Harlem, declared that the move reflected a Nazi-like mindset.

It is true that many blacks are ambivalent about preferences, or even critical of them. At the same time, however, they are highly sensitive to perceptions of white assaults on civil rights, and they may well find polemics of the Jackson and Rangel variety persuasive.

Confronted with all these obstacles, some opponents of affirmative action are leaning toward a compromise strategy involving a program-by-program review. This would be a serious mistake; the most desirable and politically effective course would be federal legislation modeled on the CCRI. Such a measure would leave in place the old laws against discrimination but would eliminate all federal programs which extend preference on the basis of race (as well as ethnicity or gender).

The measure would conceivably take the form of a reaffirmation of the sections of the 1964 Civil Rights Act dealing with the workplace, with special emphasis on the clauses explicitly prohibiting reverse discrimination. But whatever the specific shape of the new legislation, absolute clarity would be required on the principal issue: there would be no room for fudging, vagueness, or loopholes on the question of bringing the era of race-conscious social policy to a close. The legislation would therefore also have to include an explicit disavowal of the disparate-impact doctrine, under which the disproportionate representation of the races (or sexes) is often regarded as evidence in itself of discrimination, and which has often led to the imposition of de-facto quota systems.

The political struggle over this kind of sweeping legislation would be angry and unpleasant. But eliminating both the practice of racial preference and the controversy surrounding it would set the stage for an ultimate improvement in the racial environment throughout American society. On the other hand, an approach focusing on a program-by-program review of the multitude of preference initiatives in an ephemeral search for compromise only guarantees the permanence both of affirmative action itself and of the affirmative-action controversy.

A less sweeping but nevertheless useful approach would be a presidential decree revoking the executive order issued by President Johnson which opened the way to federally-mandated quotas. Though (as we have seen) Johnson did not necessarily intend this to happen, the fact is that his directive became a crucial pillar of the affirmative-action structure. With the stroke of a pen it could be rescinded.

So far as the universities are concerned, the elimination of affirmative action would mean an end to lowering standards in order to fill racial quotas. No doubt this would also mean a smaller number of blacks at the elite universities, but there are perfectly decent state colleges and private institutions for every promising student whose qualifications do not meet the standards of Yale or Stanford. The notion that a degree from one of these institutions consigns the graduate to a second-class career is based on sheer prejudice and myth; for evidence to the contrary, one need look no further than the new Republican congressional delegation, which includes a number of graduates from what would be considered second- or third-tier colleges.

It hardly needs to be added that directing a student to a university for which he is educationally and culturally unprepared benefits neither the student nor the university nor the goal of integration. The results are already clear to see in the sorry state of race relations on campus. Many colleges are dominated by an environment of racial balkanization, with blacks increasingly retreating into segregated dormitories and black student unions, rejecting contacts with white students out of fear of ostracism by other blacks, and then complaining of the loneliness and isolation of campus life. Drop-out rates for those admitted on affirmative-action tracks are high, adding to black student frustration. These problems are invariably exacerbated by college administrators who respond to racial discontent with speech codes, sensitivity training, multicultural seminars, curriculum changes, and other aggressively prosecuted diversity initiatives.

Some have proposed basing affirmative action in university admissions on social class—that is, extending preferences to promising students from impoverished backgrounds, broken homes, and similar circumstances. On a superficial level, this would seem a sensible idea. Blacks would profit because they suffer disproportionately from poverty. Universities would gain from the high motivation of the students selected for the program. And real diversity would be enhanced by the presence of students whose backgrounds differed radically from the middle- and upper-class majority, and whose opinions could not be so predictably categorized along the conformist race (and gender) lines which dominate campus discussion today.

One major caveat is that college administrators, who give every indication of total commitment to the present race-based arrangements, would discover ways to circumvent a program based on color-blind standards. Indeed, they have already done so. Under the terms of the *Bakke* case (1978), which established the guidelines for affirmative action in university admissions, race could be counted as one of several factors, including social class; affirmative action based on race alone, the Supreme Court said, could not pass muster. As matters have evolved, affirmative action on many state campuses, most notably those in California, is based almost exclusively on race and ethnicity.

A similar class-based formula is difficult to envision outside the realm of university admissions. Yet there is no reason to assume that private businesses would respond to the elimination of government-enforced affirmative action by refusing to hire and promote qualified blacks. A return to race-neutral government policies would also enable black executives and professionals to shed the affirmative-action stigma, since no one would suspect that they were in their positions only as the result of pressure by a federal agency. The supporters of preferential policies may dismiss affirmative action's psychological effects on the beneficiaries as unimportant. But the evidence indicates that the image of a black professional class having risen up the career ladder through a special racial track is a source of serious workplace demoralization for members of the black middle class.

The arguments which have lately been advanced in favor of retaining affirmative action are by and large the same arguments that were made more than twenty years ago, when the intellectual debate over preference began.

Probably the least compelling of these is the contention that the advantages extended by university admissions offices to athletes, the children of alumni, and applicants from certain regions of the country justify extending similar advantages on the basis of race. The answer to this contention is simple: race is different from other criteria. America acknowledged the unique nature of racial discrimination when it enacted the landmark civil-rights laws of the 1960s. Moreover, the suggestion cannot be sustained that outlawing preference based on race while permitting preference based on nonracial standards would leave blacks even farther behind. Blacks, in fact, benefit disproportionately from admissions preferences for athletes or those with talents in music and art. No one objects, or thinks it unusual or wrong for some groups to be overrepresented and others to be underrepresented on the basis of such criteria.

A similar, but even weaker, argument (already alluded to above) holds that America has never functioned as a strict meritocracy, and that white males have maintained their economic dominance through connections, pull, and family. Affirmative action, this theory goes, simply levels the playing field and actually strengthens meritocracy by expanding the pool of talent from which an employer draws. The problem is that those who advance this argument seem to assume that only white males rely on personal relationships or kinship. Yet as we have learned from the experience of immigrants throughout American history, every racial and ethnic group values family and group ties. Korean-American shop-owners enlist their families, Haitian-American taxi fleets hire their friends.

What about the claim that affirmative action has improved the racial climate by hastening the integration of the workplace and classroom? While the integration process has often been painful and disruptive, there is no question that more contact between the races at school and at work has made America a better society. But integration has not always succeeded, and the most signal failures have occurred under conditions of government coercion, whether through busing schemes or the imposition of workplace quotas. In case after case, the source of failed integration can be traced to white resentment over racial preference or the fears of blacks that they will be perceived as having attained their positions through the preferential track.

There is, finally, the argument that, since black children suffer disproportionately from poor nutrition, crack-addicted parents, wrenching poverty, and outright discrimination, affirmative action rightly compensates for the burden of being born black in America. Yet affirmative action has been almost entirely irrelevant to these children, who rarely attend college or seek a professional career. The new breed of Republican conservatives may sometimes betray a disturbing ignorance of the history of racial discrimination in America. But on one crucial issue they are most certainly right: the march toward equality begins at birth, with the structure, discipline, and love of a family. The wide array of government-sponsored compensatory programs, including affirmative action, has proved uniformly ineffective in meeting the awesome challenge of inner-city family deterioration.

To advocate a policy of strict race neutrality is not to ignore the persistence of race consciousness, racial fears, racial solidarity, racial envy, or racial prejudice. It is, rather, to declare that government should not be in the business of preferring certain groups over others. Because it got into this business, the United States has been moved dangerously close to a country with an officially-sanctioned racial spoils system. Even Justice Blackmun was concerned about this kind of thing. In his *Bakke* opinion, Blackmun made it clear that preferential remedies should be regarded as temporary, and he speculated that race-conscious policies could be eliminated in ten years—that is, by the end of the 1980s.

Affirmative action's supporters grow uncomfortable when reminded of Blackmun's stipulation, which clashes with their secret conviction that preferences will be needed forever. Despite considerable evidence to the contrary, they believe that racism (and sexism) pervade American life, and they can always find a study, a statistic, or an anecdote to justify their prejudice.

If racial preference is not eliminated now, when a powerful national momentum favors resolving the issue once and for all, the result may well be the permanent institutionalization of affirmative action, though probably at a somewhat less expansive level than is the case right now. Alternatively, a cosmetic solution, which eliminates a few minor policies while leaving the foundation of racial preference in place, could trigger a permanent and much more divisive racial debate, with a mushrooming of state referenda on preference and the growing influence of extremists of both races.

It is clear that a bipartisan majority believes that the era of racial preference should be brought to a close. It will take an unusual amount of political determination and courage to act decisively on this belief. But the consequences of a failure to act could haunt American political life for years to come.

RACE AND RAGE[3]

All Janice Camarena wanted, she says, was to attend English 101 at a convenient hour. For the commuting student at San Bernardino Valley College—a twenty-five-year-old widow with three young kids—the only convenient hour was 11 a.m. But there was a problem. She was white—and the section was reserved for African-Americans. Bearing a neutral label, the class was actually part of a "Black Bridge" remedial program of writing instruction, career counseling, and mentoring. She couldn't sign up.

So . . . Janice Camarena did what any red-blooded Californian would do. She sued. Now she's a test case for those who want to remove any trace of racial preference in the state's vast community-college system. The Black Bridge doesn't seem to be an egregious piece of race-based social engineering. Few would begrudge minority students special help early in college, and there were other sections of English 101. Yet Camarena's case briefly broke through the O.J. chatter on Los Angeles talk radio. "Everybody should have an equal chance," she says, "regardless of the color of their skin."

Surf's Up: The color of their skin. Never far from the surface of politics, race is rising with raging force in the presidential campaign now beginning. A quarter century ago the issue was busing.

[3]Article by Howard Fineman, staff writer, from *Newsweek* 125:22–5 Ap 3 '95.

In 1988 it was crime. . . . The floor of the House was the scene of vicious debate over welfare reform. Black Democrats hurled accusations of racism and Nazism, while victorious Republicans (the measure prevailed, 234–199) compared aid recipients to alligators and wolves.

But the most profound fight—the one tapping deepest into the emotions of everyday American life—is over affirmative action. It's setting the lights blinking on studio consoles, igniting angry rhetoric in state legislatures and focusing new attention on the word "fairness." When does fairness become "reverse discrimination"? When is it fair to discriminate on the basis of race or gender? Louder than before, Americans seem to be saying, "Never."

The issue is getting the most attention, naturally enough, in California. Colossal, diverse, the Golden State is where national trends are launched. The newest is a closely watched initiative with a PC-sounding name, the California Civil Rights Initiative. Likely to be on the state ballot . . . it would bar any form of affirmative-action preference—race, gender, ethnicity, national origin—in state hiring, contracting, or education.

California Republicans have a knack for recognizing—and methodically speaking to—the resentments of white suburbanites. Richard Nixon summarized their angst in his 1968 campaign for "law and order." In 1980, Ronald Reagan won on the strength of antitax fervor created by California's Proposition 13 tax revolt.

Now Pete Wilson, a sixty-one-year-old epitome of suburban solidity, thinks it's his turn. Last year [1994] the California governor capitalized on anti-immigration sentiment in his drive for reelection. Last month [March 1995] he announced that he would support the anti-affirmative-action initiative. Then . . . he declared he had a "duty" to seek the White House in the name of "fairness" for people who "work hard, pay their taxes and obey the law." A key to Wilsonian "fairness": abolishing racial and gender preferences.

A master surfer of political waves, Wilson landed in Washington [March 1995] . . . for a round of political chores. In his first interview in the capital, he adroitly made the requisite concessions. He wouldn't "quibble," he told *Newsweek*, with descriptions of him as a past supporter of affirmative action and minority "set-asides." He simply came to the conclusion recently that preferences were unfair and unworkable.

Maybe so, but Wilson's smooth conversion—and decision to move toward a formal presidential candidacy—underscores affirmative action's appeal to GOP politicians. They see it as a way to prove their conservative bona fides to the rank and file. They also see it as a classically divisive "wedge issue," the kind that forces your foe to choose which constituency he wants to offend—in this case, either suburban white swing voters or traditional liberals. "It's a winner for us any way you look at it," says Republican strategist Bill Kristol.

The *Newsweek* poll shows why. The chasm between blacks and whites is deep, though minorities are more dubious of preferences than the rhetoric of their most vocal leaders suggests. By a 79-14 margin, whites oppose racial preferences in employment or college admissions; minorities support them by a 50-46 margin.

Political Bleeding: The affirmative-action issue is tearing at the Democratic Party, which lost the white male vote by a breathtaking 62-36 margin in the 1994 elections. The party's right wing is in open revolt. The Democratic Leadership Council, a group of self-described moderates, has become an anti-affirmative-action cell. When he assumed chairmanship of the DLC . . . [April 1995] Senator Joseph Lieberman of Connecticut declared that race and gender preferences were "patently unfair."

The Democratic left is answering back. Rev. Jesse Jackson led a rally in New Haven . . . [March 1995] to protest Lieberman's remarks. "We submit to the senator of this state," Jackson said, "that we have marched too long, died too young, bled too profusely, been to too many funerals of young mothers, to go back now." The state's other senator, Democratic National Committee Chairman Christopher Dodd, backed Jackson's view.

Caught in the middle, the Clinton administration is doing the usual: emitting a cacophony of mixed signals. Some White House officials privately complain that GOP candidates are exploiting race. Elsewhere the administration is reviewing affirmative-action programs—and has already turned down at least one, for student interns at the Commerce Department. A major speech on the issue by President Clinton has been put off. . . . The administration sent forth its leading civil-rights attorney to defend affirmative action—but only speaking for himself. Clinton, talking earnestly to college students, yearned out loud for a way to avoid divisiveness.

Meanwhile, the Republicans are driving their "wedge." Charlie Black, top adviser to GOP contender Phil Gramm, linked the president to another California politician, the abrasively liberal Maxine Waters of Los Angeles. "In the end, Clinton will do whatever she tells him to do," Black said tartly. Jackson attacked from the other side, issuing a warning to the White House in a *Newsweek* interview. "If they sacrifice justice on the altar of expediency, we will fight back," he said. "We will not stand idly by."

Among Republicans, there's no philosophical disagreement over affirmative action. But the GOP debate could get nasty just the same, if only over the question of who says "no" with the most conviction.

Claim to Purity: Republicans are scrambling to up the anti-ante. A promise to abolish affirmative action was a centerpiece of Phil Gramm's announcement pageant. . . . Before Gramm arrived in California for a state GOP convention—Wilson announced his support for the ballot initiative. Then, . . . columnist Pat Buchanan declared his presidential candidacy in New Hampshire and staked a justifiable claim to purity. He labeled his opponents "leap-year conservatives."

The Republicans have their own man in the middle, front runner Bob Dole. The majority leader has promised to introduce legislation banning racial and gender preferences in government programs. But Dole had long supported minority set-asides, and prides himself on his civil-rights record. . . . He will host a three-hour meeting in his office to discuss a legislative course and try to do what he does best—broker a deal. Among those expected to attend: Democratic D.C. Delegate Eleanor Holmes Norton, former Bush White House counsel Boyden Gray and conservative black columnist Armstrong Williams.

That leaves Wilson, who seemed to be basking in the glow of his own possibilities. . . . White House insiders consider him the greatest threat to Clinton's re-election. Jackson has a harsher view. "He's nothing more than a sophisticated George Wallace," he told *Newsweek*. Hardly. Wilson is a social liberal in some respects, with a strong record of supporting abortion rights, gay rights and gun control. Lean and placid, carefully turned out . . . in a gray suit, the Yale-educated Wilson has always been adept at putting a bland face on middle-class anger. Voters seem to like the calm reflection of themselves he offers. It is a formula that Wilson has used to win in the past, and that he hopes to use in the affirmative-action wars ahead.

THE CALIFORNIA CIVIL RIGHTS INITIATIVE[4]

It is a distinct privilege to appear again before the Commonwealth Club. I am especially pleased on this occasion to have been invited to share some thoughts on the difficult and troubling issues of race, equality and affirmative action.

Let me begin with what could be the defining issue of the 1996 election here in California. The California Civil Rights Initiative—if its supporters can gain 616,000 signatures—will place on the 1996 election ballot a constitutional amendment prohibiting the state, its universities, its agencies or local governments from using "race, sex, color, ethnicity, or national origin as a criterion for either discriminating against, or granting preferential treatment to, any individual or group in the operation of the state's system of public employment, public education or public contracting."

Californians are already engaged in an emotional debate that has the earmarks of a religious war. Normally, voters look to their elected representatives to "reconcile the irreconcilable" through negotiation, deliberation and accommodation. But so deep are the passions and frustrations over affirmative action that the chances for the process of conciliation to turn the clash of rival views into some kind of agreement are not encouraging.

The dispute over the initiative touches the sensibilities of voters everywhere. For one thing, twenty-two other states have initiative procedures that would permit similar public votes. More immediately, both President Clinton and Democratic Party leaders are deeply worried that the anti-preference initiative will work to hurt the Democrats in their bid to carry this state next year. Polls already show that it is likely to pass by a large majority. It has the backing of the Republican Party, virtually all of the legislature's Republicans, and one independent (state Senator Quentin Kopp). However, not a single Democratic state senator or

[4]Speech delivered to the Commonwealth Club, San Francisco, CA by John H. Bunzel, senior research fellow, Hoover Institute, from *Vital Speeches of the Day* 61:530-3 Je 15 '95. Copyright © 1995 by City News Publishing Co.

assemblyman has endorsed the initiative. Uneasy and badly split, the Democrats are trying to figure out what position to take.

All of which prompts the question: Why has affirmative action ignited such a wildfire of emotions at the grass roots of California? The short answer is that "the economy, stupid" is not the only issue on the minds of Californians (or of voters anywhere). Even at a time when the economy has improved, many moral, political and cultural concerns assert themselves in voter consciousness. Affirmative action is one of them.

But there is a more fundamental reason why this issue is heading for the California ballot. A growing number of citizens, reflecting the mood of political cynicism and estrangement in the nation at large, feel that politicians and government officials have for too long turned a deaf ear to their views and sentiments. The ballot initiative is their way of signaling that they no longer want to be ministered from above by distant bureaucrats and "condescending elites" who presume to know how best to manage issues like affirmative action.

One reason the voters will find it difficult to vote against the ballot initiative is that some of its language is a paraphrase of the 1964 Civil Rights Act, which gave political sanction not to racially preferential treatment, or special privileges for some, but to the elimination of discrimination against anyone. Supporters of the initiative say they are simply seeking to restate the motives and purposes of Congress when it passed this thirty-year-old landmark legislation. They also want to let the most aggressive affirmative actionists in the federal bureaucracy and elsewhere know that their regulatory efforts to transform the meaning of equal opportunity from "fair and non-discriminatory competition" to the "achievement of numerical and racial goals" is contrary to wider public interests and opinion.

However, nothing in politics is as simple as it often seems. For that reason I need at this point to be candid with you. By instinct and habit I am a complexifier, not a simplifier. I am suspicious of "either/or" perspectives. I think it is important to keep open a skeptical eye to avoid simplistic choices and the dichotomies of true and false. Thus I believe there are legitimate procedural and substantive concerns about the proposed ballot initiative. Specifically, I feel that the Yes-or-No direct democracy of the initiative process is too blunt an instrument to shape a more deliberative and nuanced response to such a complex issue. The backers of the

initiative urge us to "Just Say No" to race preferences. By asserting the superiority of pure principle, they are calling for an absolute prohibition against any consideration of race.

But this is where things get complicated and untidy. Let me
offer you the following proposition as a way of stating all too
briefly my own analytical framework: Amidst the divergence of
assertions and assumptions, affirmative action must ultimately be
viewed in relation to other competing principles and in light of
many practical problems, which is why it often represents a colli-
sion of right versus right rather than of right versus wrong.

If I am correct, then it seems to me that many of the most ar-
dent supporters off the California ballot initiative may easily fall
into the trap of believing that affirmative action is WRONG and
the initiative is RIGHT. It is a classic zero-sum formulation.

But I would not wish to be misunderstood. Although I am
skeptical of the effort to deal with the multi-layered issues of affirmative action through a ballot initiative, I am not at all implying
any kind of blanket endorsement of affirmative action. This is
why I find it necessary to keep two or more different and often
conflicting thoughts in mind at the same time. For example, the
Supreme Court in the *Bakke* case, as well as other courts in other
decisions, have allowed race to be considered a factor in employment hiring and college admissions. Furthermore, race is a permissible consideration where a pattern of discrimination has been
discovered. But it is also true that these efforts to use race to overcome the racism of the past and the present have resulted too often in unfair practices over the past three decades.

One of the most basic and difficult questions we need to address is this: How much race should be considered in any good
faith effort to surmount the consequences of racial discrimination or, more specifically, the distinctive forms of economic and
social disability that afflict African-Americans and other minorities? The most honest answer is: No one really knows—although
most people think that race is presently considered excessively
and sub rosa. Emeritus political science professor Philip Siegelman believes that what is needed is "some way of calibrating the
relevance of race that falls between NOTHING and TOO
MUCH." It is the same problem that the courts have been repeatedly addressing—without great success. But is there any reason
to believe that those who frame the issue of affirmative action in
absolutist terms have a viable solution or (as Siegelman says) "can

accomplish with a few words on the ballot what every other institution has been unable to accomplish?"

Assume for a moment that you have been appointed to a newly created National Committee on Affirmative Action. One of many questions you are asked to consider is whether some degree of race consciousness is ever credible or defensible. I suggest that you would quickly need to focus on the central purpose and mission of different institutions in order to come up with an appropriate answer. Would you want race-based preferences to be applied where it was agreed that talent and skill are the only important considerations—for example, in choosing a brain surgeon or a quarterback for the San Francisco 49ers? I think not. In both of these cases the only criterion that really matters is ability of the highest quality. Race or color is irrelevant and unimportant. But suppose you are the police chief in a large American city. One of your many considerations might be community representation—that is, how to reach out and represent the different racial, ethnic and other groups that make up the total community. Or suppose there was an urgent need to hire a black police officer to work underground in the black community. Would you or your committee tell the police chief that in filling this position he must be completely blind to a candidate's color? And what about our political parties, which have been known to favor a "balanced ticket" when preparing to run for the presidency? Are they never to take race or gender into consideration?

Colleges and universities present different and special concerns. Any justification for race-conscious affirmative action in undergraduate admissions must at the same time identify reasoned limits as to how much is to be sanctioned. A member of an admissions committee might find it difficult to tell an audience of black high school seniors that being an athlete or the son or daughter of an alumnus are legitimate considerations for college admission but that one's race or ethnicity will never, under any circumstances, be taken into account. Someone will also point out that our universities must promote campus diversity. But are there no limits to what should be done in the name of diversity? Surely campus diversity is important, but just as surely it should not be pursued at the cost of weakening the critical and fragile idea of individual merit. It is one thing to say that some consideration of race in undergraduate admissions is credible and defensible. It is something very different, however, if a student is rejected solely because of his or her race in favor of another who is less academically qualified. What one really needs to know is whether or not student applicants are ever held to a different academic standard because of race or ethnicity.

I am thinking out loud here, trying to balance different claims and interests and to develop a theory of limits. Thus I believe in the central importance of the *individual*, which therefore leads me to be deeply skeptical about the relevance of *group* identity in the admissions process. Yet I am also prepared to say that race, ethnicity and gender are not trivial aspects of a person's identity, especially in this era of heightened sensitivity to such matters. Consider a practical problem: Should a university admissions committee oppose the uniform use of race *per se* in *every* consideration of admissions because, for example, some black students have not been disadvantaged by virtue of their race if they have gone to Exeter and have come from upper middle class families? Or this very different question: If some black students know they have been given preferential admissions *because of* their race, isn't it a strong possibility—some would say virtually inevitable—that they will demand the campus respond to them in racial terms once they are present?

When it comes to the recruitment of faculty, the issues are qualitatively different. Here I would insist that the most important and uncompromisable objective should be to hire the best qualified person on the basis of academic preparation and qualifications. What is not supportable is a straight racial line in making faculty appointments to meet some pre-determined goal.

These are only some of the difficult issues and actual conditions that the initiative process does not address. How many times have you and I been asked if we are "for" or "against" affirmative action? My answer has always been, "What kind of affirmative action?" The term by itself has no innate meaning—or, to put it another way, it is a term that can mean many different things. I was an early supporter of affirmative action when it was intended to further equal opportunity and to end discrimination, and when it was also promoted as a way of contributing to the larger social good of integrating women and minorities into a society that for too long had been unwelcoming. But I am very critical of what affirmative action has *become*—critical in particular of the present results-oriented form of affirmative action which imposes a standard of group identity that judges people more by their group membership rather than as individuals, and encourages the kind of preferential treatment that employs pre-set and race-based numerical goals (the functional equivalent of quotas) in hiring and promotion.

This is not a semantic quibble. One kind of affirmative action is opportunity-related. The other is not. That is why these terms need to be carefully defined. As Earl Raab, founding member of the Human Rights Commission in San Francisco, has observed, the problem with proposed laws and initiatives that do not define and qualify their terms is "that the benign and necessary is thrown out along with the malign and misplaced." Why do so many Californians favor the 1996 civil rights ballot initiative? Principally because they believe it may be the only chance they will have to hit the politicians and bureaucrats over the head with a two-by-four to get their attention.

Let me pause briefly to tell you about a special evening I enjoyed a few years ago. Early in the 1992 presidential campaign I was invited to a small dinner party here in the San Francisco Bay Area for Bill Clinton. For the dozen or so who were present, including both Republicans and Democrats, it was a rare opportunity to have several hours of quiet conversation during which we asked Mr. Clinton his views on a wide range of issues. Among those we discussed were some of the problems entangled with the politics of equality and affirmative action. Stressing his belief in equal opportunity, he left no doubt that if elected president he would conduct all-inclusive and non-discriminatory searches for the most highly qualified persons he could find for positions in his administration. He also agreed that government should not mandate an equality of results, which is why he was opposed to quotas that foster racial, gender or ethnic preferences—the same position taken by the Democratic Leadership Council in 1991 when he was its chairman. The hope was expressed that evening that if he became president, he would take the lead in providing fresh ideas on these issues—for example, by calling for affirmative action to be refocused so that it would be based more on economic need than on race, and also by defining his basic principles and social values *before* the Republicans tried to do it for him.

Then-Governor Clinton's understanding of these sensitive and complex issues was reassuring to a long-standing (but increasingly independent) Democrat like myself who has been critical of both Republicans and Democrats for what Senator Bradley has called the "silence of distortion" that has shaped the issue of race and race relations for too long. Unfortunately, however, Mr. Clinton chose not to engage in any public discussion of affirmative action during the first two years of his presidency. Only in the last month [May 1995] or so—and only then in response to the proposed ballot initiative here in California and public sentiment reflected in national polls—has he finally ordered a complete review of affirmative action. But it was not initiated on his own terms or by his own choice.

The question now is whether President Clinton will confront the dilemma facing the Democrats not only in California but throughout the nation: how to respond to pressure from the liberal-left wing of the party, including civil rights and minority group leaders on the one hand, and, on the other, how to deal with the fear that the party's continuing identification with quotas, preferential benefits and reverse discrimination will alienate both the traditional base of white working class support and the pivotal middle class as well. Bear in mind that up to now he and the Democrats have largely avoided the awkward and tough issues centering around race- and gender-based preferences, a silence that has strengthened the hand of conservative Republicans who, as House Speaker Newt Gingrich recently acknowledged, never were fully engaged in the struggle for civil rights in the '40s, '50s, and '60s.

A good way for President Clinton to begin his review would be to recognize the concerns that have formed the basis of public opposition to the direction affirmative action has taken. For example, he could point out that at various intellectual levels Americans not only believe in equality for individuals but are also committed to the long-standing system of values that emphasizes individual merit, personal liberty, hard work and competitive achievement. Properly understood, this is a view of equality built on a sequence of ideas that runs from equality before the law, to equality of opportunity, and only then to an equality of outcomes.

At the political level, the President could confirm the need to question old thinking and old solutions. The civil rights agenda has changed, and many of the government's past actions no longer represent the best approach to improving the conditions of America's blacks and other minorities. Instead of viewing politics as a "zero-sum, race-reductionist game" that leads to division and confrontation, we need to develop strategies that seek "deracialized" solutions to fundamental socio-economic problems.

White House Chief of Staff Leon Panetta says that President Clinton "clearly opposes moving backwards on affirmative action." But would it really be a move backwards for the President to recognize that it is not just "angry white males" who want to change the preference-driven policies of affirmative action? A recent *Wall Street Journal*/NBC News survey reported that 61 percent of all adults "favor eliminating affirmative action based on race or gender in college admissions, hiring for governmental jobs, and awarding federal contracts." Here in California, the latest Field poll showed that 59 percent of women voters favor the ballot initiative, as do 42 percent of African Americans.

I would go even further. I think it would be a major step *forward* if the President were to acknowledge openly that opposition to numerical preferences, race-specific targets, or statistical goal-setting for minority improvement is often founded (as Harvard professor Nathan Glazer has pointed out) "on a liberal vision as devoted to equality as that of its opponents," and is, in fact, more a reflection of general principle than of racism. Wouldn't it also be a mark of leadership if President Clinton were to say to Willie Brown, California's Democratic Assembly Speaker, that he does not speak for most Californians—or for most people across the country—when he dismisses as racists those who oppose race- and group-based preferences in hiring or college admissions? Does anyone really believe it is racist to urge admissions officials to target for recruitment disadvantaged students with poorer socio-economic backgrounds *regardless* of their race?

This is a crucial distinction that President Clinton fully understands. We should not be surprised, therefore, if he finally decides that affirmative action should be redirected to give more consideration to a person's economic need and circumstances than to race or ethnicity. After all, surveys have shown for over twenty years that the American people consistently support special aid programs that enable disadvantaged women and minorities to increase their skills and opportunities and thereby "catch up to the standards of competition set by the larger society." Stated simply, they approve of *compensatory action* to help make up for past discrimination based on race, sex, poverty, or other grounds. What Americans do not support is *preferential treatment*—not just quotas, which are opposed by almost everybody, but any form of absolute preference.

It seems clear to me that we now need to move beyond affirmative action as we know it today and develop new and more constructive approaches to the severe problems that still demand recognition and amelioration. This will not be easy. The massive institutional arrangements of affirmative action have reached into almost every corner of our society. What do we put in its place? We certainly cannot argue against *something* with *nothing*. When slavery was abolished, people were set free—but as my colleague Professor Siegelman reminds us, we did not step away from the moral and political questions that freedom brought. We needed the 13th and 14th amendments, and in our lifetime we needed the 1964 Civil Rights Act. If the analogy is appropriate, then the efforts to refocus affirmative action should signal the necessity of readdressing the problems that presumably contributed to the inequalities and injustices which brought affirmative action into being in the first place.

As an educator, I have believed since the early 1970s that affirmative action was spending too much time and energy on the wrong end of the pipeline. For example, too often—not always, but too often—ill-prepared black students who are admitted to universities under some preferential auspices do not make it academically. They drop out. Not *all* black students, but too many. We need to be honest here. A poorly educated young person who has not had an adequate support system at home and who has not been socialized to an educational environment is almost surely not going to be converted into a successful college graduate. Believing otherwise is one of the misguided expectations of affirmative action.

What, then, is the *right* end of the pipeline? I can only suggest here the beginning of an answer that reflects a special concern. I believe any serious reformulation of approaches and strategies should make clear that special preferences and race-based numerical goals will not help dismantle the cycle of despair and destruction that produces an underclass in our society. The most promising hope lies in longer-term efforts—for example, in a fundamental rearrangement of expenditures (or even an increased expenditure) to improve on a vast scale the quality of education in our inner cities through early Head Start programs, financial incentives for students, teachers and successful schools, and expanded apprentice programs that combine classroom instruction and on-the-job training. Through these and other programs, offered to all who are less privileged regardless of race or color, perhaps we can provide more promising grade and high school students the kind of education that would make preferential admissions and reverse discrimination at the college level superfluous.

I am talking about real changes. Instead of adult remedies that are twenty or thirty years too late, we need strong and affirmative intervention at an earlier stage of a young person's development. This is not a new idea—but it remains a good idea (although insufficiently implemented) that deserves our strongest consideration. Yes, it will presumably cost more money, which means that charting a different course will not be easy. But I believe it will also do more good than harm, and will certainly create less bitterness and division. The major problem with affirmative action today is that instead of bringing us together as originally intended, it has pulled us apart. I know of no more important or urgent task facing all of us than trying to rebuild the national consensus on equal rights and equal justice so that we can move a step closer to fulfilling the promise made long ago of equal protection for all Americans.

AFFIRMATIVE ACTION ON THE ROPES[5]

It is called the California Civil Rights Initiative (CCRI), and if enacted, it would end affirmative action in California. The state and its subdivisions would be prohibited from using race, color, sex, ethnicity, or national origin to discriminate against or grant preferential treatment to any individual or group.

The result would be no set-asides for minority contractors, no special admissions programs for colleges, no race-based hiring in government jobs. In a state in which an estimated five thousand white men were told recently that they could not take the qualifying test for the Los Angeles Fire Department until it met its minority and gender hiring goals, the CCRI has become the wedge issue.

[5]Article by Nicolaus Mills, author and editor, from *Dissent* 42:189–90 Spr '95. Copyright © 1995 by *Dissent*. Reprinted with permission.

For California Governor Pete Wilson, who used his support of Proposition 187, the referendum that would deny most publicly funded services to illegal aliens, to win a come-from-behind victory over liberal Kathleen Brown, the CCRI may even be the issue that makes him a presidential candidate. After months of testing the California political waters, Wilson has formally endorsed the initiative. "I don't think that it's fair to give preferences based on race or gender," he declared when asked about the CCRI. "I think that what we should do is make those judgments based upon merit after affording real equality and opportunity of success."

The CCRI is the brainchild of Thomas Wood, the executive director of the conservative California Association of Scholars, and Glynn Custred, an anthropology professor at California State University at Hayward. Their headquarters are in a tiny office on Martin Luther King, Jr. Way in Berkeley, but the smallness of their operation belies the importance the CCRI has for California and the nation. No other single piece of legislation promises so clear a referendum on American politics in the nineties.

Last year [1994] the CCRI was introduced in the State Assembly by Republican Bernie Richter of Chico. It died in the Judiciary Committee. At the time it was opposed by both the black and Hispanic caucuses, and in 1995 it is certain to have their opposition again. Liberal anger with the initiative runs deep. As Eva Paterson, the executive director of the Lawyers Committee for Civil Rights in San Francisco, observed in an interview in the *Washington Post*, "You can call it Willie Horton goes to college."

Wood and Custred are not worried about the initiative being defeated in the State Assembly. They believe that political momentum is on their side and that the passage of Proposition 187 by such a wide margin shows that voters are angry and willing to take matters into their own hands.

It will take 616,000 signatures to get the CCRI on the ballot for 1996, but given the interest the initiative has already aroused, that task can be easily accomplished with enough financing. The initiative has the support of such conservative Republicans as William Buckley and Pat Buchanan, as well as former Secretary of Education William Bennett.

Republicans are increasingly confident the CCRI will force the electorate to choose between them and a Democratic party wedded to minority preferences. Their confidence is easy to understand. The Civil Rights Act of 1991 notwithstanding, current support for affirmative action hangs by a thread. A *Wall Street Journal*/NBC News survey found that two out of three Americans oppose affirmative action, and according to a *Los Angeles Times* poll, 73 percent of Californians support the CCRI.

The best case for affirmative action was made thirty years ago by President Lyndon Johnson as the South's Jim Crow laws were being dismantled. "You do not take a person who, for years, has been hobbled by chains," Johnson declared, "liberate him, bring him up to the starting line of a race and then say, 'You are free to compete with all others' and still justly believe you have been completely fair." What Johnson had in mind by way of fairness were the job training and education programs of the *Great Society*. In the prosperous 1960s there was no sense that affirmative action might be a zero-sum game in which one group's gain was another group's loss.

However, since the 1960s affirmative action has come to be a zero-sum game for many. At the 95,000 companies employing the twenty-seven million workers covered by federal affirmative action programs, the policy often means hiring one person over another in order to meet a mandated goal. A parallel situation is true for colleges, where in the name of diversity a student with lower test scores and grades is often accepted over one more academically qualified. To make matters worse, with the passage of time it has become increasingly difficult to determine who deserves the preference affirmative action brings. Does the black youngster from the suburbs merit extra consideration? If so, what do we say to the unemployed mineworker's son from West Virginia who may have received a far worse education?

The result is that opinion on affirmative action tends to break down along many of the same racial and ethnic lines that divide American society. Those who see themselves benefiting from affirmative action regard it as a social necessity. Those who see themselves being hurt by it regard it as unfair. It is hardly surprising that a *New York Times*/CBS poll found that 71 percent of blacks, as compared to just 17 percent of whites, favor affirmative action.

The CCRI thus presents Democrats and Republicans with very different challenges. At stake for the Democrats is their ability to win major elections. They can oppose the CCRI and become still further identified as the party of minorities in America. Or they can break with their past and declare that the time has come to replace affirmative action with a more inclusive liberalism in which real equality—beginning with identical funding for suburban and urban schools—becomes the goal of social policy. The problem is that the longer Democrats wait to make such a break with their past, the less likely the decision is to strike voters as principled. Before affirmative action is buried at the polls, Democrats need to begin negotiations for the programs that would replace it by reaching out to all in need.

For Republicans, on the other hand, the CCRI provides every incentive to stay with the politics of meanness that brought them into power in 1994. They have already made the welfare and balanced-budget issues theirs. If they can do the same with affirmative action, they will have redefined the politics of the decade. What is more, they will have done so by taking from the Democrats the moral ideal on which the Civil Rights Act of 1964 and the Voting Rights Act of 1965 rest—the belief that we are a colorblind nation in which racial entitlements have no place.

II. CONGRESS AND THE COURTS

Editor's Introduction

Section Two deals with pending legislation in Congress and recent decisions in the courts. In an article in *U.S. News & World Report*, Steven V. Roberts sees a massive attack being mounted against affirmative action by Republican legislators, whose opposition has been emboldened by their party's successes in the 1994 congressional election. Recent polls reveal that affirmative action is opposed by two out of three Americans. Commenting on the Washington scene, Holly Idelson, in *Congressional Quarterly Weekly*, remarks that affirmative action programs giving women and minorities special consideration for federal contracts and jobs have been particularly controversial. It also appears that Senate majority leader Bob Dole, who had previously supported affirmative action will sponsor legislation to undo most federal efforts. Big business, however, seems unlikely to abandon affirmative action entirely, having come to embrace the concept of diversity in the workplace.

Reporting on affirmative action and the legal system in *BusinessWeek*, Catherine Yang notes that Deval Patrick, chief of the Justice Department's Civil Rights Division, has been drawing fire from the Republican right. In a recent decision, Patrick forced Chevy Chase Federal Savings Bank to spend $11 million to open up branches and offer low-interest loans in black neighborhoods it had refused to service. Reacting to such decisions, the Clinton administration has appointed Deputy White House Counsel Joel I. Klein as watchdog on Patrick's office. "Anything that can smack of quotas," Yang writes, "could get Patrick caught up in a tempest." In the next article, Evan Thomas writing in *Newsweek* discusses a recent ruling of the U.S. Supreme Court in the case of *Adarand v. Pena*. When the Adarand construction company lost out to a Hispanic-owned company under a program that earmarked highway contracts for minorities, Adarand's owner filed suit. In a 5–4 decision, the high court sided with Adarand, applying a legal test that will make it difficult to preserve government programs that give an edge to minorities and women. The case seems a portent of others to come, as affirmative action, once considered invulnerable, continues to fall into disfavor.

Tony Mauro and Tom Watson in *USA Today* discuss the effects affirmative action is having on the court system as a whole. There was a time when the courts fully supported affirmative action and preferences being given to minorities. However, recent rulings show that the courts have had thoughts about reconsidering. "They've muddied the waters, but they haven't yet turned 180 degrees," says Elaine Jones of the NAACP.

In the concluding article, reprinted from *The New Republic*, Jeffrey Rosen discusses a case involving the admissions policy of the University of Texas law school that seems headed for the Supreme Court. The case, according to Rosen, is the most important challenge to racial preference in university admissions since the *Bakke* decision in 1978, which struck down a set-aside-for-minorities program at the University of California-Davis medical school. The University of Texas's rationale was that without racial preferences only one out of the 280 applicants to the law school in 1992 had a test score high enough to be presumptively admitted. Because of this, the school created an advisory committee to consider applications from African- and Mexican-Americans separately, and accepted lower scores for admission. The admission score for minorities dropped to 189, three points below the rejection score for whites.

AFFIRMATIVE ACTION ON THE EDGE[1]

Affirmative action is a time bomb primed to detonate in the middle of the American political marketplace. Federal courts are pondering cases that challenge racial preferences in laying off teachers, awarding contracts and admitting students. On Capitol Hill, the new Republican majority is taking aim at the Clinton administration's civil rights record. On the campaign trail, several Republican presidential hopefuls are already running against af-

[1]Article by Steven V. Roberts, staff writer, from *U.S. News & World Report* 118:32-5 F 13 '95. Copyright © Feb. 13, 1995 by *U.S. News & World Report*. Reprinted with permission.

firmative action. And in California, organizers are trying to put
an initiative on next year's ballot banning state-sanctioned
"preferential treatment" based on race or gender.

This increasingly angry and divisive debate about the role of
race and gender in modern America could help the Republicans
unseat Bill Clinton in 1996 and change the way many institutions
allot jobs, business and benefits. A recent *Wall Street Journal*/NBC
News survey found that two out of three Americans, including
half of those who voted for President Clinton in 1992, oppose affirmative action. The *Los Angeles Times* found 73 percent of Californians back the ballot initiative. "The political implications are
enormous," says Will Marshall of the Democratic Leadership
Council, a moderate group. "Obviously, a lot of Republicans look
at affirmative action as the ultimate wedge issue."

The assault on affirmative action is gathering strength from
a slow-growth economy, stagnant middle-class incomes and corporate downsizing, all of which make the question of who gets
hired—or fired—more volatile. Facing attacks on such a broad
front, women's groups, civil rights organizations, and other defenders of affirmative action are circling their wagons. Women
and minorities still need preferential treatment, they argue, because discrimination still exists, causing blacks and other minorities to lag far behind whites in terms of economic status. "If
African-Americans are taking all these jobs," asks Barbara Arn-
wine of the Lawyers Committee for Civil Rights Under Law,
"why is there double-digit unemployment in the African-
American community?" Adds Patricia Williams, a professor at
Columbia Law School: "There is this misplaced sound and fury
about nothing. Access is still very limited, and the numbers are
still very low."

But the sound and fury are real. Affirmative action poses a
conflict between two cherished American principles: the belief
that all Americans deserve equal opportunities and the idea that
hard work and merit, not race or religion or gender or birthright,
should determine who prospers and who does not. In 1965, Lyndon Johnson defended affirmative action by arguing that people
hobbled by generations of bias could not be expected to compete
equally. That made sense to most Americans thirty years ago, but
today many argue that the government is not simply ensuring
that the race starts fairly but trying to decide who wins it.

Moreover, many women and racial minorities are no longer disadvantaged simply because of their race or gender. Indeed, most of the young people applying for jobs and to colleges today were not even born when legal segregation ended. "I'll be goddamned why the son of a wealthy black businessman should have a slot reserved for that race when the son of a white auto-assembly worker is excluded," says a liberal Democratic lawmaker. "That's just not right."

Disheartening. The critics of affirmative action include some conservative minority and women's leaders who believe it has a destructive effect on their own communities. Thomas Sowell, the black economist, argues that affirmative action has created a process of "mismatching," in which competition for talented minorities is so fierce that many are pushed into colleges for which they are not ready. "You can't fool kids," says Linda Chavez, a Hispanic activist. "They come into a university, they haven't had the preparation, and it's a very disheartening experience for some of them."

Others say affirmative action causes co-workers to view them with suspicion. "White skepticism leads to African-American defensiveness," says Sharon Brooks Hodge, a black writer and broadcaster. "Combined, they make toxic race relations in the workplace." Glenn Loury, an economics professor at Boston University, says proponents of affirmative action have an inferiority complex: "When blacks say we have to have affirmative action, please don't take it away from us, it's almost like saying, 'You're right, we can't compete on merit.' But I know that we can compete."

William Bennett, former education secretary and a leading GOP strategist, says that "toxic" race relations, aggravated by affirmative action, have led to a damaging form of re-segregation: "Affirmative action has not brought us what we want—a colorblind society. It has brought us an extremely color-conscious society. In our universities we have separate dorms, separate social centers. What's next—water fountains? That's not good, and everybody knows it."

But supporters of affirmative action maintain that arguments like Bennett's are unrealistic—even naive. "We tried colorblind thirty years ago, and that system is naturally and artificially rigged for white males," says Connie Rice of the NAACP Legal Defense and Education Fund. "If we abandon affirmative action, we return to the old-boy network."

Voices on both sides of the debate are starting to discuss a possible compromise that would focus eligibility on class, instead of on race or gender. For example, the son of a poor white coal miner from West Virginia would be eligible for special help, but the daughter of a black doctor from Beverly Hills would not. "Some of the conventional remedies don't work as one might have hoped," says University of Pennsylvania law professor Lani Guinier, whose ill-fated nomination as Clinton's chief civil rights enforcer sparked a storm of protest from conservatives. "Perhaps there is an approach that does not suggest that only people who have been treated unfairly because of race or gender or ethnicity have a legitimate case."

No one questions the sensitivity of the subject. For years, the civil rights lobby, backed by Democrats in Congress, was so strong that critics often felt intimidated. Even today, Democrats who disagree with affirmative action are reluctant to voice their doubts. "The problem is political correctness—you can't talk openly," says a member of Congress.

Democrats *are* talking privately, however, urging the White House to formulate a response to the anti-affirmative action wave before it swamps the president and the party. At the Justice Department, chief civil rights enforcer Deval Patrick is ready: "We have to engage; we can't sit to one side."

But despite the fact that the California initiative could cost Clinton a must-win state in 1996, the administration seems sluggish, even paralyzed. Laments a senior adviser, "We're going to wait until it's a crisis before reacting." White House political strategists admit one reason for the inaction: The issue is a sure loser.

Referee? Caught between angry white males and the party's traditional liberal base, White House advisers think the best they can do is position the president as an arbiter between two extremes. In a recent interview with *U.S. News*, the president voiced his aim this way: "What I hope we don't have here, and what I hope they don't have in California, is a vote that's structured in such a way as to be highly divisive, where there have to be winners and losers and no alternatives can be easily considered." Asked his views on affirmative action, the president tried—as he often does—to please both sides: "There's no question that a lot of people have been helped by it. Have others been hurt by it? What is the degree of that harm? What are the alternatives? That's a discussion we ought to have."

But a senior administration official admits that the middle ground will be an uncomfortable place: "The civil rights groups are going to say we're caving in if we make any compromises. And the Republicans are going to shout, 'Quotas.'" That same tension is already developing within the White House. *U.S. News* has learned that Chief of Staff Leon Panetta is quietly asking friends on Capitol Hill whether the president should simply endorse the California initiative—a position sure to trigger outrage among the president's more-liberal advisers.

Unsure how resolute the White House will be, civil rights groups are looking for their own strategy to defend affirmative action. One of their main jobs, they say, is to debunk the "myth" that unqualified women and minorities are being hired in large numbers. And some of the best salesmen for affirmative action are big corporations that adjusted long ago to the demands for a more-diverse work force, dread bad publicity and fear the uncertainty change would produce. James Wall, national director of human resources for Deloitte & Touche LLP, a management consulting firm, says diversity is good business: "If you don't use the best of all talent, you don't make money."

Even so, the combination of old resentments, new economic hardships and shifting political winds threatens to explode. "There's a great deal of pent-up anger beneath the surface of American politics that's looking for an outlet," says conservative strategist Clint Bolick of the Institute for Justice. It's the same anxiety that helped pass Proposition 187 in California, which sharply restricts public assistance to the children of illegal immigrants, and thwarted Clinton's plan to push a Mexican aid plan through Congress. "If there is a squeeze on the middle class," says GOP pollster Linda Divall, "people get very vociferous if they think their ability to advance is being limited."

Some African-American leaders insist that this white-male anger is being stirred up by demagogues who make blacks and women into scapegoats. Says Derrick Bell, professor of law at New York University: "There is a fixation among so many in this country that their anxieties will go away if we can just get these black folks in their place."

But the anxieties are strong and are coupled with a growing belief that affirmative action is another aspect of intrusive and inefficient big government. "The real back-to-basics movement is not in education but in politics," says William Bennett. "We're rethinking basic assumptions about government."

Accordingly, the fight over affirmative action is playing out in four arenas:

• **California.** The real question is whether the civil rights initiative will appear on the primary ballot in March of 1996 or on the general-election ballot. If it appears in November, the measure could seriously damage President Clinton's chances to carry the nation's most populous state. That is precisely why national Republicans are promising to raise money for the effort—as long as organizers aim for November.

The initiative is the brainchild of two academics, Tom Wood and Glynn Custred, who say they were alarmed by the prevalence of "widespread reverse discrimination" in the state's college system. The initiative has already attracted some unlikely support: Ward Connerly, a black member of the University of California Board of Regents, said . . . that he favors an end to racial and gender preferences. "What we're doing is inequitable to certain people. I want something in its place that is fair." And Hispanic columnist Roger Hernandez wrote: "I've never understood why Hispanic liberals, so sensitive to slights from the racist right, don't also take offense at the patronizing racists of the left who say that being Hispanic makes you an idiot."

California Assembly Speaker Willie Brown, who is black, opposes the initiative as an attempt "to maintain white America in total control." But other Democrats are scurrying for cover. "The wedge potential is absolutely scary," says Ron Wakabayashi, director of the Los Angeles County Human Rights Commission. "The confrontation of interests looks like blacks and Latinos on one side and Asians and Jews on the other."

• **The Courts.** The Supreme Court has generally supported race and gender preferences to remedy past discrimination, but an increasingly conservative bench has moved to limit the doctrine. In 1989, the Court struck down a program in Richmond, VA, that set aside 30 percent of municipal contracts for racial minorities, and that decision set off a flurry of litigation. In the current term, the Court already has heard arguments in a key case: A white-owned construction company is claiming that it failed to get a federal contract in Colorado because of bonuses given to contractors that hire minority firms.

In another case making its way toward the high court, a black teacher in Piscataway, NJ, was retained while an equally qualified white teacher was fired, in the name of diversity. The Bush administration sided with the white teacher after she sued the school board. The Clinton administration backs the board. Two other cases relating to education are also moving forward. In one, white students at the University of Maryland are challenging a scholarship program reserved for minorities. In the other, the University of Texas law school is being sued for an admissions policy that lowers the standards for blacks and Hispanics.

While most court watchers do not expect sweeping changes in current doctrine, the high court is closely divided on racial-preference questions, and the deciding votes could be cast by Justice Sandra Day O'Connor. Legal analysts cite her opinion in a 1993 case challenging voting districts that were drawn to guarantee a black winner: "racial gerrymandering, even for remedial purposes, may balkanize us into competing racial factions." The court's most likely move: require programs to be more narrowly tailored to remedy past discrimination.

• **Congress.** Republican victories last year [1994] mean that critics of affirmative action now control the key committees and the congressional calendar. A strategy session was held . . . at the Heritage Foundation, a conservative think tank, bringing together about two dozen Hill staffers, lawyers, and conservative activists. Already, Representative Charles Canady, the Florida Republican who heads the key House subcommittee, has written to the Justice Department requesting every document relating to affirmative action cases. His goal: oversight hearings that try to demonstrate that the administration's civil rights policies far exceed the original intent of Congress.

Conservatives are considering amendments to appropriations bills that would restrict the administration's flexibility. There also is talk of a measure banning racial and gender preferences altogether. Civil rights proponents remain confident that Clinton would veto any measure that eviscerates affirmative action and that his veto would survive.

• **Campaign 1996.** The affirmative action issue will be test-marketed . . . by Buddy Roemer, a Republican candidate for governor of Louisiana. But it is already intruding into the politics of 1996: California Governor Pete Wilson has all but endorsed the initiative and Senator Phil Gramm of Texas, who will soon announce his presidential candidacy, has taken over the appropriations subcommittee that handles the Justice Department. He will use it, predicts an administration official, "as a platform to rail against quotas."

The danger for Republicans lies in going too far in attacking affirmative action and courting resentful white males. If the anti-affirmative-action campaign "turns into mean-spirited racial crap, to hell with it," William Bennett warned fellow Republicans.

But the questions at the core of the affirmative-action debate remain unanswered. How much discrimination still exists in America? And what remedies are still necessary to aid its victims?

PRESSURE BUILDS FOR RETREAT ON AFFIRMATIVE ACTION[2]

Senator Joseph I. Lieberman, D-Conn., disregarded affirmative action critics in 1991 and supported a job discrimination bill that they said would lead to hiring quotas for women and minorities. But he has grown increasingly sympathetic to arguments that affirmative action has gone too far. "It's been building in me," Lieberman says of his concern. "We have to find another means" to ensure equal opportunity.

Lieberman is one of a growing number of moderate lawmakers who are rethinking affirmative action and helping to throw its future into question. The political tremors are felt in California, where an anti-affirmative-action ballot initiative is roiling state politics and where Governor Pete Wilson announced June 1, 1995 that he was curtailing controversial programs. The tremors reach to the White House, where President Clinton has ordered a review of federal programs that give special consideration to women and minorities. And in Congress, Republicans are leading an even more aggressive push to re-examine and perhaps roll back affirmative action laws.

Several policies are under fire, from race-conscious redistricting for political elections to minority scholarships. But it is affirmative action in the workplace—policies such as numerical goals and timetables to move women and minorities into certain jobs—that appears to be generating the most concern. There is particu-

[2]Article by Holly Idelson, staff writer, from *Congressional Quarterly Weekly Report* 53:1578–82 Je 3 '95. Copyright © 1995 by *Congressional Quarterly Weekly Report*. Reprinted with permission.

lar agitation over government programs that give women and minorities special consideration for federal contracts and jobs, and lawmakers are expected to at least trim these programs.

The debate could heat up . . . . Charles T. Canady, R-Fla., who chairs a House Judiciary subcommittee with responsibility for civil rights, is poised to introduce legislation erasing virtually all federally sponsored affirmative action. The Supreme Court is due to rule on a case involving federal contracting by summer, and the Clinton administration nearly has completed its affirmative action review.

Affirmative action has withstood numerous past assaults, however, and the current criticism may not be sufficiently deep or focused to prompt an overhaul. Big business, for example, generally has grown to accept affirmative action.

"We feel diversity is critical," says Johanna Schneider, a spokeswoman for the Washington office of the Business Roundtable, a group of large-company executives. "CEOs think it's the right thing to do and it only makes sense." Moreover, some GOP leaders have yet to specify what changes they would like to see in employment and contracting policies that aim to promote women and minorities.

Still, members are at least talking seriously about doing away with officially sanctioned preferential treatment or replacing race- and gender-conscious programs with those targeting poor people.

Opponents of affirmative action say either that it has worked so well that it is no longer needed or that it always has been an ill-conceived effort that promotes women and minorities at the expense of more qualified white men. They say that ongoing affirmative action will exacerbate racial and gender divisions in society and lead to a balkanized polity.

Advocates insist that affirmative action has worked and has yet to outlive its usefulness. Any substantial retreat, they argue, will invite a resurgence of discrimination.

Antipathy toward affirmative action is driven in part by economic unease, as well as by resentment that newly arrived immigrants may be eligible to participate in such programs.

Yet some activists on both sides say the biggest change is not economic or demographic, but political: It has become more acceptable to criticize affirmative action. Where most political leaders once supported affirmative action even in the face of considerable popular skepticism, many of these leaders are hostile or at least questioning.

"The difference is the perception in political circles," says Linda Chavez, president of the Center for Equal Opportunity, a conservative think tank, and an opponent of affirmative action. "A lot of politicians seem to have suddenly discovered that these programs are preference programs."

Alternately, some defenders of affirmative action say critics are distorting the facts—falsely equating affirmative action with quotas and overstating the incidence of reverse discrimination—to exploit public apprehension.

Rep. John Conyers Jr., D-Mich., a senior black lawmaker who supports the programs, puts it this way: "It's just people making the most of a sensitive issue that people can get some political mileage out of."

New Attitude

Some of the current tensions about affirmative action surfaced during congressional debate on the 1991 civil rights legislation (PL 102-166) that made it easier for workers to sue for job discrimination. An early version went down amid criticism that it was a "quota bill" that would force employers to hire women and minorities according to strict ratios.

The 1994 elections brought a clearer opportunity to challenge affirmative action, simultaneously signaling a more conservative electorate and putting some affirmative action skeptics in charge of key congressional posts.

Presidential politics have helped prod opponents into high gear, as Clinton and the Republican contenders jostle for position on the issue. The controversial ballot proposal to undo affirmative action programs in California—a key electoral state in national politics—ensures that the issue will figure in the 1996 presidential race.

The Republican Party has long included strong critics of affirmative action, so it is not surprising that members' success in the 1994 elections would embolden them to attack. Even Senate majority leader Bob Dole, R-Kan., who has supported affirmative action, is now critical and may sponsor legislation to undo most federal efforts.

Many Democrats have been strong supporters of the policy, reflecting its importance to minority and women's groups, which are among the party's most steadfast allies.

Yet elements of the Democratic coalition, such as working-class whites, have been uncomfortable with affirmative action for years. And now Clinton and other key Democrats seem to be struggling to find a proper stance on the issue.

Clinton has said he still supports affirmative action and is looking to improve rather than abandon it. Even that is considered a betrayal by some within the party, where liberal politicians are bracing to defend the embattled programs. Key Democrats, such as House minority leader Richard A. Gephardt of Missouri and Senator Christopher J. Dodd of Connecticut, while publicly welcoming the review, have pledged ongoing support for affirmative action.

But Lieberman, who chairs the centrist Democratic Leadership Council, said he and some colleagues are increasingly hard put to reconcile the notion of group preferences with the ideal of individual opportunity.

"That inconsistency has become more and more evident over time and has become less and less tenable politically," he says. "I think the current system cannot stand."

Pressure Points

The term "affirmative action" embraces a range of initiatives, including special recruiting, goals and timetables for hiring or promoting minorities and women, as well as rules to allot a portion of government contracts for minority- or female-owned companies.

There is little dissent over recruiting and outreach programs for women and minorities, which make up a large portion of affirmative action efforts. On the other end, policy-makers also unite against fixed hiring quotas, which are unlawful in virtually all contexts.

The friction comes over whether race or gender should factor into hiring and firing decisions. For example, is it sometimes appropriate to look beyond pure test scores and give an extra plus to a diversity candidate? What about set-asides in government grants or procurement rules?

Lawmakers' differing responses to such questions reveal large gaps in the way discrimination and affirmative action are perceived.

Studies indicate that affirmative action has helped to move women and minorities into traditionally segregated professions, although these studies differ on the impact of the gains. Yet Chavez and other critics insist that the policies have taken a far greater toll on individual fortunes and societal values than can be set off by any gains they may have provided.

They see affirmative action as a departure from principles of meritocracy and individual striving and as a policy that costs white men who may have had no part in any past or present discrimination.

Hiring quotas are illegal, but critics say managers are nonetheless "hiring by the numbers" to avoid discrimination lawsuits. And over time, such perceived or real abuses have accumulated. "I think more and more people are being impacted by affirmative action," says House Judiciary Committee Chairman Henry J. Hyde, R-Ill.

Critics also charge that many affirmative action programs benefit only a few, privileged minorities or women rather than helping the truly disadvantaged. Early in 1995, Republicans eagerly attacked a tax credit for companies that sell television and cable stations to minorities. The tax break figured in plans by Viacom, a media and entertainment giant, to sell its TV systems to a black-owned company and defer millions in taxes—a scenario many lawmakers decried as far removed from the guiding aspirations of the civil rights movement.

These criticisms appear to resonate with voters, white men in particular. Some women and minorities also have voiced ambivalence toward affirmative action, arguing either that it is unneeded or that it is harmful because personal achievements may be attributed to "preferences" rather than merit.

But some policy-makers are bitter about calls for a meritocracy in which race and gender would play no role. It is precisely because the qualifications of some women and minorities have been slighted, they say, that affirmative action is important. "How do we go back to this colorblind society when we didn't have it in the first place?" asked Rep. Donald M. Payne, D-N.J.

Advocates say affirmative action forces employers to scrutinize the explicit or hidden biases that can close opportunities for women and minorities. They say everyone benefits from this broadening: Employers get a more diverse work force, and white men may have more opportunities when employers go beyond the "old boy network" to hire based on objective factors.

To a great extent, the current fight revolves around whether that kind of hiring has become the norm and would exist without affirmative action.

AT&T, for example, has been under a consent decree since 1973 to promote more women and minorities. Spokesman Burke Stinson says what began as an exercise in court-ordered compliance has now become a way of doing business. "The concept of including people, no matter their race, creed or color, is now pervasive," he says.

Rep. Harris W. Fawell, R-Ill., who has conducted hearings on affirmative action as chairman of the Economic and Educational Opportunities Subcommittee, says most employers today look for the most qualified worker, regardless of race or gender. He says that while his grandparents undoubtedly discriminated, "my children and my grandchildren don't. . . . They just can't be held accountable for those societal wrongs" of earlier generations.

But Conyers says many critics are too quick to see discrimination as a thing of the past. "It's easy to think things are better than they are."

Deval Patrick, head of the Justice Department's civil rights division, told members of a House panel that they would be "astonished and saddened" by the egregious cases that continue to land on his desk. In 1994, Patrick says, the Equal Employment Opportunity Commission (EEOC) received 91,000 complaints of job discrimination. And a recent study by the Glass Ceiling Commission indicated that white men still hold the vast majority of upper-level jobs.

Supporters do not embrace proposals to recast affirmative action to help those who are economically disadvantaged. Civil rights advocates say such efforts should be made in addition to affirmative action, not in place of it.

"Affirmative action was never meant to be an anti-poverty program," says Ralph G. Neas, a veteran civil rights lobbyist who is coordinating a pro-affirmative action campaign for the Leadership Conference on Civil Rights. "It enabled people who were discriminated against to have an equal opportunity."

Muddied Field

During the 1991 legislative debate, civil rights groups had positive momentum as they sought to overturn or restrict the effect of several Supreme Court decisions that were seen as unfairly burdening plaintiffs in job discrimination suits.

This round, they are on the defensive while affirmative action critics appear to have the upper hand. "Clearly the ground has shifted," says Chavez.

Just throwing a spotlight on affirmative action may help generate opposition to the programs.

Seymour Martin Lipset, a public policy professor at George Mason University, says that many politicians in the past avoided the issue for fear of opening themselves to charges of racism or sexism. Now that events like the California ballot initiative have placed affirmative action on the table, political sentiment favors at least some retrenchment. "The politicians now find it hard to resist," Lipset says.

But opponents' newfound momentum does not automatically translate into legislative success.

The simplest action would be to scale back or eliminate federal programs that give special consideration to women and minorities. These include hiring requirements or incentives for federal agencies, grant recipients, and federal contractors.

These federal programs affect many jobs and serve as a signal to other employers on affirmative action issues. Many lawmakers and policy analysts consider it likely that Clinton, Congress, or both will support some adjustments in this area.

Canady's bill would eliminate such programs and also would seek to restrict programs ordered by the federal courts in response to proven discrimination.

However, Congress cannot alter voluntary affirmative action programs in the private sector or by state and local governments unless lawmakers are prepared to rework the 1964 Civil Rights Act.

Hyde and others say that is a complicated proposition and one that Congress may not have the stomach for—especially absent a strong, organized lobbying effort.

That sort of campaign has yet to materialize. Religious conservatives are more focused on other social issues, such as school prayer and abortion. Nor is the business community clamoring for lawmakers to act.

Women, who arguably have benefited more than minorities from affirmative action, also represent a large political force to block or limit revisions. Many national women's groups have expressed vehement opposition to a rollback of affirmative action, although polls suggest women voters are more equivocal.

Such political uncertainty—and a packed legislative calendar—have raised hurdles for the issue in Congress. However, the issue is heating up in the race for the Republican presidential nomination—a race that includes Dole, Senator Phil Gramm of Texas, and Senator Richard G. Lugar of Indiana—and could easily spill over into the Senate. Jesse Helms, R-N.C., has introduced bills to outlaw preferential treatment on the basis of race or gender. Canady's legislation should help focus attention on the matter in the House.

Clint Bolick, a conservative activist who has been working with lawmakers on the issue, predicts that legislation to end federally sponsored affirmative action will pass both chambers.

For their part, affirmative action supporters acknowledge that they have plenty of work ahead to bolster political and popular support for their cause, but remain optimistic their position will improve as the focus shifts from the abstract to the specific.

"I am confident that a bipartisan majority will defeat efforts to undo affirmative action," says Neas.

Chavez, from a different viewpoint, says Neas may be right. "I've spent too many years in this to think it's an easy battle," she says. "This is a long haul."

THE EDUCATION OF DEVAL PATRICK[3]

Deval L. Patrick didn't see it coming. In one of his first major moves as chief of the Justice Dept.'s Civil Rights Div., Patrick forced Chevy Chase Federal Savings Bank [in the] summer [of 1994] to spend $11 million to open up branches and offer low-interest loans in black neighborhoods it had refused to service.

[3]Article by Catherine Yang, staff writer, from December 12, 1994 issue of *BusinessWeek* 92-4. Copyright © 1994 by The McGraw-Hill Companies. Reprinted with permission.

Bankers were outraged because the thrift hadn't discriminated against any loan applicants. They denounced the ease as extremist and complained that Justice was overstepping the law. "Patrick was surprised by our strong reaction," says industry official Kenneth A. Guenther.

To assuage his critics, the Civil Rights chief invited ten top bankers to discuss the controversial case. A rare droll moment in the $2\frac{1}{2}$ hour meeting . . . came when a squeaky cart rolled by the meeting room. One of the executives joked that it was the body of another banker going by.

Treading Lightly. So goes the painful political education of Deval Patrick. And the thirty-eight-year-old former corporate lawyer is likely to face a lot more rough spots in the months ahead. At his post . . . , Patrick must delicately implement a civil-rights agenda without making the already vulnerable Clinton administration look like it's bending over backwards for minorities. Upcoming issues are potentially explosive, such as one challenging college scholarships reserved for minorities. "Anything that can smack of quotas could get Patrick caught up in a tempest," notes John P. Relman, a public-interest civil-rights lawyer in Washington.

Patrick knows he has to tread lightly. But he's optimistic that civil rights can flourish, particularly in areas such as voting rights, lending discrimination, and bias against the disabled. "We view ourselves as a law-enforcement office, not a law-reform office," Patrick says. After the conservative sweep in November 1994, Patrick sent his staff an inspirational E-mail message telling them not to despair. But some aides are worried. "The administration doesn't want us to do anything that will turn into a bumper sticker in 1996," grumbles one Justice lawyer.

The political climate is so dicey that a watchdog of sorts is overseeing Patrick's office. Since this fall, Deputy White House Counsel Joel I. Klein has been reviewing significant affirmative action cases now before the government. He says the administration is trying to work out "a consistent, coherent view" of affirmative action that could distance the President from the dangerous "quota" label. Some controversial cases may reach the Supreme Court during the 1996 Presidential election campaign. "The line between quotas and forms of legitimate actions can be thin," says White House Counsel Abner J. Mikva. "It's important that they be separated out." Patrick declines comment on Klein's new watchdog role.

The Civil Rights chief is certainly viewed more moderately than Clinton's first choice for the civil-rights post, University of Pennsylvania law professor Lani Guinier. Her nomination in 1993 was dropped after conservatives labeled her a "quota queen" for her academic writings. With Patrick, who was sworn in during April [1994], the Clintonites got a clean-cut, moderate-sounding Boston corporate lawyer with a compelling life story. He grew up poor on Chicago's South Side after his saxophone-player father ran off to join jazz musician Sun Ra when Patrick was just four years old. He went to the prestigious Milton Academy on scholarship and then to Harvard College and Law School. He worked a short stint as a civil-rights advocate at the NAACP Legal Defense & Educational Fund before joining Boston law firm Hill & Barlow.

"Outrageous." But nothing in his background prepared him for the Washington limelight. GOP lawmakers already are calling for hearings on several of Patrick's decisions. Some of his moves "appear to be outrageous," railed incoming Senate Judiciary Committee Chairman Orrin G. Hatch, R-Utah, in a recent TV interview.

Exhibit No. 1 for conservatives is Patrick's friend-of-the-court brief filed in an affirmative-action case at the U.S. Court of Appeals in Philadelphia. Patrick reversed the Bush administration's position in support of a white teacher who was fired by the Piscataway, NJ, school board in favor of a black teacher who had the same seniority and qualifications. Patrick argued that employers should be free to use affirmative-action goals to determine which of two equal candidates to terminate. Otherwise, private employers could be prevented from voluntarily integrating their workforces. "Piscataway is not a quota case," says Patrick.

But the decision has set off a furor on the right. "It suggests this administration is back to playing the numbers game in civil rights," charges Clint Bolick, vice-president of the conservative Institute for Justice. If the charge sticks, Patrick's moves could give conservatives more ammunition. According to a poll . . . by the National Opinion Research Center, 54 percent of Americans are against special treatment for minorities, while only 16 percent are clearly for it. Even though Clinton and Patrick both oppose quotas, the Republicans are still likely to try to score points on the issue.

Brave Face. There already are signs that the administration is getting more cautious. Two days after the election, it declined to support the University of Maryland's scholarship program for black students. The university wants a rehearing of an appellate court decision that ruled the program unconstitutional. Initially, the Education Dept. recommended siding with the university, says a Justice attorney. But the administration hasn't backed up the university's request for a rehearing a move that school advocates contend is aimed at pleasing middle-class voters. "If there was a decision not to pursue the case, it was a political one," says Janell M. Byrd, a lawyer for the NAACP Legal Defense & Educational Fund. Patrick declines comment on the case.

Despite Patrick's brave public face, friends say that he was stung by the fallout from the *Piscataway* case. But they insist that he can withstand the shifting political currents. Days after the election, Patrick called Hatch and joked that he had barely had time to congratulate the senator on his new committee chairmanship before the attacks against him began. Still, Patrick is keenly aware that he's in a hot spot. "Being a lightning rod takes getting used to," he concedes. "If I walked on water, certain of my critics would still say that Patrick can't swim." If he wants to avoid sinking, Patrick will have to keep not only the law but also politics foremost in his mind.

RETHINKING THE DREAM[4]

Few white men have better civil-rights credentials. The old newspapermen who had gathered for an informal reunion at the Atlanta airport Holiday Inn . . . had been thrown in jail and chased out of dusty delta towns during the Movement Days of the 1950s and '60s. During a night of strong drink and reminiscence, the old hands from publications like the *New York Times* and the *Washington Post* quietly recalled the clarity of the clash between peaceable black demonstrators and the Bull Connors of the then

[4]Article by Evan Thomas, staff writer, from *Newsweek* 125:18-21 Je 26 '95. Copyright © 1995 by Newsweek, Inc. Reprinted with permission. All rights reserved.

segregated South. "Hell, everything was clearer then," said Claude Sitton, who covered the region for the *Times* from 1958 to 1964. "Going to the back of the bus, drinking out of separate water fountains, going to segregated schools—those are the kinds of things that just hit you right between the eyes." But in the morning, the aging veterans puzzled over the current state of the civil-rights struggle—the tedious court battles over formulas and standards. "When it gets down to all of the subtleties and complexities of legal tests, well, that's much harder for the public to understand," said John Popham, a dapper octogenarian who covered the first stirrings of the movement for the *Times* back in the late 1940s. No one came out and said it, but there was a sense that the revolution they courageously covered may be losing its indisputable moral force.

Conservative politicians have been criticizing affirmative action for years. What's different today is that the once liberal establishment has begun, grudgingly and slowly, to have its own second thoughts. The judges and unelected executive-branch officials who have largely made affirmative-action policy for the past twenty-five years—and the editorial writers who have supported them—are beginning to back off. They eschew the rhetoric of Republican presidential candidates who want to make affirmative action a "wedge" issue. The establishment would like to find a comfortable compromise. That's difficult, as President Clinton is discovering. Promised months ago, the administration's review of government affirmative action is still a work in progress, with no end in sight. But over time, the likely effect of such second-guessing will be to largely remove the government from handing out jobs or contracts or school admissions based on race.

. . . The U.S. Supreme Court seemed to scale back the federal government's own affirmative action. By a 5–4 vote, the justices fashioned a legal test that will make it very difficult, if not impossible, to preserve government programs that give an edge to minorities and women. The decision in *Adarand Constructors v. Pena* was written in the usual murky legalese. But the point was articulated by the plaintiff, Randy Pech, whose Adarand construction outfit in Colorado had lost out to a Hispanic-owned company under a program that earmarked highway contracts for minorities. The burly Pech asked why he should be discriminated against to make up for discrimination that occurred more than a century ago.

Reaction to the decision was muted. Of course, civil-rights leaders are angry; Rev. Jesse Jackson called it a "major setback." But except for the *New York Times*, there was little protest on op-ed pages. A White House spokesman blandly noted that the administration was "asking many of the questions the Court focused on."

The decision signals that the high court is following the election returns. For more than a decade, since it ruled that race could be a "factor" in university admissions in the 1978 *Bakke* case involving the University of California, the Court had basically rebuffed challenges to affirmative action. In recent years, however, the Court has shown a growing reluctance to use "race-conscious remedies"—the practice of trying to overcome the effects of past discrimination by helping minorities and women. This has been true not only in affirmative-action cases involving jobs and contracts, but in school desegregation and voting rights as well. On the same day the Court handed down the *Adarand* decision, it also cast strong doubt, in a Kansas City, MO, case, on whether federal courts can promote integration by requiring the state to fund inner-city "magnet schools." . . . The Court is expected to curtail the drawing of racially "gerrymandered" congressional districts designed to elect minority lawmakers.

The animating notion of affirmative action has always been that it is necessary to use race to overcome the effects of racism. In some ways, the policy has worked. Affirmative action's cultural impact is unlikely to be reversed entirely—the search for minorities for jobs is now ingrained, at least informally, in many institutions. On a pocketbook level, a 1995 study by Rutgers professor Alfred Blumrosen found that five million minority workers and six million women have better jobs today than they would have had without preferences and anti-discrimination laws. Certainly, minority contractors who stand to lose from the Court's *Adarand* decision are understandably anxious. "The reality is that 90 percent of the work that we do is in the public sector," said Nigel Parkinson, president of a Maryland construction company. The decision he said, will "just kill us."

"Beyond Racism": At the same time, affirmative action has engendered tremendous resentment among whites, few of whom have lost jobs to minorities, but many of whom think they have. The policy that was supposed to get "beyond racism" risks creating more racists. Court-ordered busing did not produce integration; whites fled the inner cities, leaving schools more segregated than ever. The Kansas City program challenged in the Supreme Court spent $1.3 billion to lure suburban whites to urban magnet schools. But after a decade, the city schools were still two-thirds black.

The rule of unintended consequences is particularly ironic in the voting-rights area. The Voting Rights Act of 1965 guaranteed minorities the right to vote—but did little to increase the number of minority representatives in Congress. The Justice Department responded by encouraging states to draw some majority-minority districts. By 1993, this led to historic gains for the black and Hispanic caucuses. But the weird, serpentine-shaped districts siphoned off liberal voters from other districts—producing conservative congressmen likely to be unsympathetic to minorities.

Impatient with the important but inevitably slow progress of the courts, GOP leaders vow to pass a law that would eliminate all "racial preferences" from federal hiring and contracting. Given the public mood, it's not surprising that Senate majority leader Bob Dole and his presidential rival Senator Phil Gramm are attacking racial preferences. More telling of the shift in the establishment center was the recent scene in the Senate Labor Committee, where Nancy Kassebaum of Kansas, a moderate, held hearings to warn that affirmative-action requirements on business can become "harmful and unfair."

Diverse World: The private sector's response to all this? Most Fortune 500 companies say they are committed to affirmative action. Creating a diverse work force, they say, is good business in an increasingly diverse world. But most of these companies now work under federal rules that make sure they follow through. And many companies also have federal contracts that require them to hire minorities and women in rough proportion to the local population. Even if the Feds [government] go all the way and eliminate their requirements, some sort of affirmative action, however informal, is likely to remain. But without the standards that grew out of the '60s, affirmative action's future is a bit hazier—and diversity will depend not on clear federal action but on corporations, and people, doing the right thing.

COURT GROWS CRITICAL WHEN
RACE, LAW INTERSECT[5]

For the third time . . . during June [1995], the Supreme Court . . . said it was tired. Tired, that is, of the traditional approaches to remedying the national problem of race discrimination. On June 12, 1995 the Court's conservative majority voiced dissatisfaction with affirmative action and school desegregation.

. . . It was race-based redistricting that got the Court upset. Using race as the primary reason for creating a district, to enhance chances of electing a minority candidate, violates the constitutional guarantee of equal treatment of all races under the law, the Court said. That pronouncement, which throws hundreds of congressional, state, and local districts nationwide into turmoil, must have given pause to retired Justice Harry Blackmun, who was in the courtroom . . . to hear it.

It was seventeen years ago that Blackmun penned the simple formulation that describes the underlying theory of the approach to civil rights that the current Court is repudiating. "In order to get beyond racism, we must first take account of race," Blackmun wrote. Under that banner, the Court embraced affirmative action, which takes race into account by giving minorities preferences in contracts and employment. It endorsed special measures for minority students in schools and it encouraged remedies under the Voting Rights Act aimed at boosting the voting power of minorities.

But now, riding the same wave that brought the Republican majority to Congress last fall [1994], the Court seems to be saying that racial preferences are an idea whose time has passed. In Baton Rouge, LA, one of the areas affected by . . . the ruling, opinion seems as divided as it is within the Court.

A. J. Lord, owner of A. J.'s Restaurant, agrees it is important to have minorities in Congress. But he also believes other things are just as important, such as having members of Congress represent cohesive districts. Louisiana's 4th District was drawn to create a majority-minority district, but it is so far-flung, says

[5]Article by Tony Mauro and Tom Watson, from *USA Today* Je 30 '95. Copyright © 1995 by *USA TODAY*. Reprinted with permission.

Lord, that many voters don't know who their congressman is. "At some point, you have to weigh your objectives to elect black candidates to office, or have proper representation of a district," says Lord. "It's a balancing act and there's no easy solution."

Frank Ransburg, a political scientist at Southern University, a historically black school in north Baton Rouge, says abolishing the district now represented by Rep. Cleo Fields, who is black, would reverse important civil rights gains. "There are some people in the state who don't feel that blacks should be allowed to fully participate in the political process," Ransburg says. Most liberals say the Court is too hasty in declaring the problem of racial bias solved, and that race-conscious remedies are no longer needed.

"The three decisions reflect unfortunate judicial resistance to reasonable efforts toward racial inclusiveness," says Harvard law professor Laurence Tribe. "The combined effect is to turn the clock back on an effort that is not yet completed." The Reverend Jesse Jackson: "The Court has authorized the country to unravel the legal fabric of social justice and inclusion that has been woven together over the last forty-one years." Jackson has special words of contempt for Justice Clarence Thomas, the Court's only black justice, who was part of the 5–4 majority in all three cases. "It is especially painful that a descendant of slaves, in effect, stabbed Dr. (Martin Luther) King . . . in the back, and is paving the way back toward slavery," Jackson says.

The idea of drawing districts to pull in pockets of minority voters developed in the last two decades in response to a political truth: Black candidates are rarely elected in districts where whites form the majority of the population. "There are thousands of redistricting plans in the South and throughout the country in which racial fairness was taken into account," says Lauglin McDonald of the American Civil Liberties Union. "All of these plans are presumed to be unlawful."

Others in the civil rights movement are more optimistic, especially after the Court announced . . . that it would take up two new redistricting cases in the fall on related issues of race. "They've muddied the waters, but they haven't yet turned 180 degrees," says Elaine Jones of the NAACP Legal Defense and Education Fund. "The issue has just begun."

Clinton administration civil rights chief Deval Patrick, whose department reviews redistricting plans under the Voting Rights

Act, says, "It would be a tragedy if these decisions led to the rese-
gregation of American democracy."

IS AFFIRMATIVE ACTION DOOMED?[6]

On September 7, 1994 Deval Patrick, the assistant attorney
general for civil rights, filed a brief in a New Jersey case arguing
that it is legal to fire a white teacher over a black teacher purely
because of her race. And on August 19, 1994 a federal district
judge in Austin, TX, held that aspects of the affirmative action
program at the University of Texas law school are unconstitutional. One or both of the cases may reach the Supreme Court before long. Each on its own could revive the debate about racial
preferences and ventilate their more troubling assumptions. Together, they suggest that the current legal foundations of affirmative action are highly unstable. If some kind of argument for
racial preferences is to be sustained at all, it has to come from
new—and more candid—premises.

For nearly a decade the Supreme Court has said that affirmative action in college and law school admissions is generally permissible; but firing someone on account of race crosses a crucial
line, for it imposes all the burdens of racial preferences on a single white victim. By challenging this distinction, which is widely
accepted by liberals and conservatives, Deval Patrick has committed the Clinton administration to a vision of racial preference
that fulfills the most extravagant fantasies of a conservative attack
ad. ("You lost that job because you were white. . . . ") Rather
than honestly confronting the costs of affirmative action, Patrick
has blithely endorsed the most extreme form of racialism. And
principled liberals in the administration are concerned. Assistant
Attorney General Walter Dellinger, for example, argued strenu-
ously against Patrick's position.

The facts of the New Jersey case, *Taxman v. Piscataway*, make
it a particularly unfortunate platform for Patrick's crusade. A

[6]Article by Jeffrey Rosen, staff writer on legal affairs, from *The New Republic*
211:25-28 O 17 '94. Copyright © 1994 by *The New Republic*. Reprinted with permission.

white teacher, Sharon Taxman, and a black teacher, Debra Williams, were hired on the same day in 1980 to teach typing and secretarial studies at Piscataway High School. In 1989 the Piscataway school board decided, in the face of budget cuts, that it couldn't afford both Taxman and Williams. Ordinarily, when two teachers are equally senior, the board flips a coin. But in this case, it decided that since Williams was the only black teacher in the business education department, she should be retained and Taxman fired. What makes the decision so peculiar is that there is no scarcity of black teachers at Piscataway High School. On the contrary, 10 percent of the teaching staff is black, nearly twice the percentage of blacks eligible to teach in the county. In firing Taxman and retaining Williams, the school board had decided that it was important to maintain racial diversity within the department of secretarial studies itself. This is the radical end-point of the diversity argument: the notion that all races should be proportionately represented, not on the faculty as a whole, but in each department of every high school in the district.

The most disappointing aspect of Patrick's brief is the coyness with which it calls into question the basic principles of the Supreme Court's affirmative action doctrine. Patrick's first innovation is his argument that "faculty diversity" is a sufficiently compelling interest to justify firing people on the basis of race. In a letter to the editors of TNR, Patrick argues that "many Supreme Court justices" have described faculty diversity as a "laudable" goal. He neglects to mention, however, that no Supreme Court majority has ever endorsed this view.

Patrick is also less than frank when he claims that "nothing in the controlling case law" clashes with his position. In fact, Justice Lewis Powell's plurality opinion in the 1986 *Wygant* case explicitly rejected the argument that white teachers could be fired over black teachers "to provide role models for minority children." Carried to its logical conclusion, Powell said, the idea that black students are better off with black teachers could lead to the very system the Court rejected in *Brown v. Board of Education*. More pointedly still, Powell objected that the role model theory allows the board to use racial preferences "long past the point required by any legitimate remedial purpose."

Patrick dismisses Justice Powell's concerns. Citing the dissenting opinion in *Wygant* by John Paul Stevens, he argues that there are a number of reasons why schools that have never discriminated in the past might seek racially diverse faculties. "It is one thing for a white child to be taught by a white teacher that color, like beauty, is only 'skin-deep,'" wrote Stevens. "It is far more convincing to experience that truth on a day-to-day basis." The argument may be intelligible for social studies teachers; but Stevens never suggested that students would benefit from being exposed to racial diversity in typing and accounting classes.

In any event, the "faculty diversity" argument is a red herring, since Justice Powell said explicitly that it is not compelling enough to justify firing people on the basis of race. Patrick argues that the Piscataway school board did not "unnecessarily trammel" Taxman's rights. But in fact, the board violated Taxman's right to have the same chance of keeping her job as anyone with equal seniority. The coincidence that Taxman and Williams were hired on the same day doesn't change the constitutional principle: in a random, colorblind system, each would have had a 50 percent chance of keeping her job. "We're not taking a position on whether this is constitutional," Patrick told me on the telephone; but his brief takes a very strong position. It explicitly rejects Justice Powell's central insight in *Wygant*: "While hiring goals impose a diffuse burden, often foreclosing only one of several opportunities, layoffs impose the entire burden of achieving racial equality on particular individuals, often resulting in serious disruption of their lives. That burden is too intrusive."

Patrick tries to minimize Taxman's injury with a series of evasions. Race, he says, "played no greater weight in the board's decision than any other qualification." This is ludicrous: as the Justice Department acknowledged before it switched sides in the case—it had originally supported Taxman rather than Williams—race was the *only* factor that tipped the scales. "Let me assure you once again, Sharon, that this board action is not related to any assessment of your professional performance," wrote Gordon Moore, the director of staff personnel, when he fired her. Patrick also argues that Taxman's injury was only "temporary," because she was rehired in 1990. (She was fired again in 1991, and then rehired the following year.) In fact, the judge calculated her lost income and benefits as $134,000—hardly a "temporary" loss.

There's something a little glib, finally, about Patrick's characterization of Supreme Court precedents. He invokes William

Brennan's opinion in the *Metro Broadcasting* case, which said that Congress could set aside FCC licenses for minority broadcasters. But Brennan went out of his way to stress that the program didn't disturb anyone's vested rights or legitimate expectations. Patrick also skims over the *Johnson* and *Weber* cases, which say that racial preferences are permissible only when they're temporary, and intended to remedy the effects of past discrimination, or to eliminate a "manifest imbalance" in the racial makeup of a workplace as a whole. The *Taxman* case meets none of these criteria.

Patrick's attempt to rewrite the law of affirmative action, rather than prudently withdrawing the government's brief in this explosive case, must be ranked among the most peculiar decisions of the Clinton Justice Department. "We do not support quotas," Patrick said when he filed the *Taxman* brief, but "affirmative action is a different animal." But when whites are fired because of their race, the euphemistic distinction between affirmative action and reverse discrimination becomes impossible to sustain. As Samuel Issacharoff of the University of Texas argues, if there is any point at which liberals should balk at racial preferences, the *Taxman* case presents it squarely.

The University of Texas case is the most important challenge to racial preferences in university admissions since the *Bakke* decision in 1978, which struck down a rigid set-aside program at the U.C.-Davis medical school; and it may give the Court another chance to re-examine the boundaries of its affirmative action doctrine. While Justice Powell in *Bakke* coyly refused to look behind the curtains of the Harvard College affirmative action program, which he praised as a model, Judge Sam Sparks of the U.S. District Court in Austin unblinkingly revealed the raw data—grade point averages and law school admission test scores—that separate white, black and Mexican-American applicants to the University of Texas. The numerical gap between the groups is so stark that it undermines the central premise of *Bakke*: that race may be used as a tie-breaker in admitting similarly qualified candidates, but that using race as a decisive consideration is "discrimination for its own sake."

With *Hopwood v. Texas*, history has made an awkward circle. In 1950 Thurgood Marshall represented Heman Sweatt, who sued the University of Texas law school because it barred blacks; four decades later four white plaintiffs are suing the same law school because it is too welcoming to blacks. In the 1940s Texas tried to resist integration by setting up a makeshift "separate but equal" law school in the basement of the state capitol; in the 1990s Texas tried to guarantee integration by imposing separate admissions standards for blacks and whites. And there are plenty of ironies from the decades in between. As late as 1980 the Department of Health, Education and Welfare found that Texas had failed to eliminate the vestiges of segregation. When the university pledged to increase the numbers of black and Hispanic graduate students in 1982, Ronald Reagan's assistant secretary of education, Clarence Thomas, rejected the plan. The numerical goals, Thomas said, were simply too low to satisfy Title VI of the Civil Rights Act of 1964. Texas, in short, finds itself trapped between what federal law requires and what the Constitution forbids.

The plan that Thomas eventually endorsed is the genesis of the plan that Cheryl Hopwood, a white, working-class graduate of a Texas junior college, challenged. Under the Texas plan, which was developed by moderate and conservative faculty members, the law school pledged to admit blacks and Mexican-Americans in proportions approaching their graduation rates from Texas colleges. Each class, the admissions committee decided, should be approximately 5 percent black and 10 percent Mexican-American.

The problem, put starkly, is that Texas cannot begin to achieve its goals without adjusting its admissions standards. The admissions committee relies heavily on a number called the Texas Index, which is a weighted average of every applicant's LSAT score and undergraduate GPA, and which has proved—both sides concede this—to be a reliable predictor of first-year grades. The school, with its first-rate faculty and low tuition, is highly selective: in 1991 white students admitted to Texas had a median LSAT in the 93 percentile and an average GPA above 3.5. In 1991 white Texas applicants with Texas Index scores above 199 were presumptively admitted, while those with scores below 192 were presumptively rejected.

The university's lawyers began the trial by frankly conceding that, without racial preferences, only one out of the 280 black applicants to Texas in 1992 had a score high enough to be presumptively admitted. Out of all the minority applicants to all the law schools *in the country*, only 289 blacks, and ninety-six Mexican-

Americans, had scores high enough to put them in the discretionary zone for white applicants to the University of Texas; and only eighty-eight blacks, and fifty-two Mexican-Americans, *in the country* had scores higher than the median for white students at the University of Texas. If the law school had based its 1992 admissions on a strictly colorblind standard, the entering class of five hundred students would have included, at most, nine black and eighteen Mexican-American students, all of whom were being courted by the most prestigious law schools in America.

Faced with the prospect of returning to a nearly all-white class (which would have been illegal under Title VI), the University of Texas balked. It established a separate admissions committee to consider applications from blacks and Mexican-Americans; and it imposed lower scores for admission and rejection. The presumptive admission score for the preferred minorities dropped to 189, three points lower than the presumptive rejection score for whites. Consequently, a score in the range of 189 to 192 was a presumptive rejection for a white applicant but a presumptive admission for a black or Mexican-American applicant.

The gap between the scores of black and white applicants is worrying on several levels. And it exposes the three central fallacies underlying the *Bakke* opinion: that race can be a plus factor rather than a decisive factor in admissions decisions; that the need for racial preferences will soon disappear; and, most implausibly of all, that only institutions with a history of discrimination are permitted to avail themselves of racial preferences today.

To be consistent with Powell's opinion in *Bakke*, Judge Sparks said, the law school had to compare black applicants to white applicants at every stage, rather than considering both sets of applications on racially segregated tracks. The procedural requirement comes from Powell's opaque notion that racial preferences in universities "must be limited to seeking the educational benefits that flow from having a diverse student body and to addressing the present effects of past discriminatory practices." But what Powell meant by the educational benefits of a diverse student body has never been clear. He seemed to be saying that a university could use race as a rebuttable presumption that a black applicant would contribute to intellectual diversity; but that admissions officers would have to decide, on a case-by-case basis, whether a given white applicant would bring *more* diversity to the mix. For example, Powell seemed to suggest, an Italian-American farmboy who had overcome great hardships might have a legitimate constitutional objection if he were rejected in favor of a son of the black middle class.

Accurately applying the vague standards of *Bakke*, Judge Sparks held that the lack of individual comparison between white applicants and minority applicants makes the Texas procedure unconstitutional. After *Bakke* was decided in 1978 the law school initially had concluded that its use of two separate tracks for minority and white applicants was unconstitutional, and decided to merge the separate committees into a single unit. But during the 1980s, Texas, like many other top law schools, such as Stanford, got sloppy and decided that it would be more efficient to revive the separate minority admissions committee once again. The persistence of separate minority committees, despite Powell's explicit prohibition, shows how little influence *Bakke* has had on affirmative action as it is actually practiced.

After the *Hopwood* suit was filed, however, Texas administrators became more careful about appearances. "When one gets sued in federal court, it catches one's attention," the admissions director testified. For the 1995 entering class, the law school has eliminated the minority subcommittee and the presumptive admission and rejection scores. All admissions decisions will be made by a single committee of three faculty members. The new, unified admissions procedure, Judge Sparks emphasized, is perfectly constitutional under *Bakke*, which is why the law school is properly treating the decision as a victory.

But the victory is incoherent. The only practical effect of *Bakke*, as correctly applied by Judge Sparks, is to punish schools that have the courage to be honest. The court is saying, in effect, that Texas can rely on the same strong racial preferences that it did before, as long as it doesn't *overtly* adopt separate admissions standards. But it's hard to see why it should be constitutional to do covertly what is unconstitutional when done openly. Furthermore, by making its separate admissions standards explicit, rather than inviting three faculty members to apply racial preferences in secret, Texas was trying to minimize the possibility for abuse.

The procedural distinction on which Justice Powell and Judge Sparks place so much weight—the distinction between separate admissions committees and a single admissions committee—collapses in light of the admissions data. The gap between the scores of black and Mexican-American candidates and other candidates is so persistent that it is simply not possible to compare minority candidates with white candidates on a case-by-case basis, and to weigh race and ethnicity in "competitive consideration" with other, nonracial qualities. In order to admit meaningful numbers of black and Mexican-American students, race must be used not as a "plus factor" but as the decisive factor, and a black professor's son will have to be preferred to a less privileged white working-class applicant—like Cheryl Hopwood—in case after case. The *Hopwood* data suggest, therefore, that the consequence of a purely class-based affirmative action policy would be virtually all-white colleges and law schools.

The *Hopwood* case highlights yet another fallacy of *Bakke*: Powell's notion that racial preferences would be short-lived. In a new biography of Powell, John C. Jeffries Jr. reveals that during the Court's private conference about *Bakke*, John Paul Stevens and Powell agreed that racial preferences might be acceptable as a temporary measure, but not as a permanent solution. Perhaps, Stevens suggested, blacks would not need preferences for much longer. At this point Thurgood Marshall broke in. Racial preferences would be necessary, he said, for another hundred years. Powell was speechless. Afterward, Powell's clerk speculated that if Marshall had predicted ten years rather than a hundred, Powell might have provided a fifth vote for the liberal's unqualified approval of racial preferences. Powell simply recoiled at the prospect of generation after generation of racial quotas.

But the evidence presented at the *Hopwood* trial suggests Marshall was right and Powell was engaging in wishful thinking. Sixteen years after *Bakke*, the gap between the scores of white and black applicants remains so persistent that it is hard to believe things will improve anytime soon. In an amicus brief submitted to the *Bakke* Court, the Association of American Law Schools pointed out that in 1976, 20 percent of white law school applicants, but only 1 percent of black and 4 percent of Chicano applicants, had LSAT scores of 600 or more and GPA's of 3.25 or higher. Without strong racial preferences, therefore, the number of black students admitted to law schools in 1976 would have been about 1 percent of the entering class. This is roughly the same as the percentage actually admitted to law schools in 1964, and it is similar to the University of Texas's estimate of the percentage that would have been produced by a colorblind admissions process in 1994. "Certainly, an indefinite program would violate the equal protection clause," Judge Sparks declared confidently; but in light of the lack of progress after thirty years, it's hard to share his optimism that racial preferences will end anytime soon.

The *Hopwood* case exposes one last fallacy of *Bakke*: the impossibility of measuring and addressing, with any precision, the present effects of past discrimination. Faced with a choice between two coherent theories of affirmative action, Powell chose neither. On the one hand, William Rehnquist, now joined by Antonin Scalia and Clarence Thomas, argues that the Constitution is colorblind and that all racial classifications are unconstitutional. Rehnquist, Thomas and Scalia would allow racial preferences only in the narrowest circumstances, as compensation from an institution that is guilty of discriminating to an individual who has been discriminated against. Although this theory is rhetorically appealing, it is flamboyantly inconsistent with the original intentions of the framers of the 14th Amendment, who considered, and rejected, language that would have prohibited racial classifications in all circumstances.

The most liberal position is also unsatisfying. According to William Brennan, Thurgood Marshall and Harry Blackmun, the Constitution forbids racial classifications only when they reflect prejudice or contempt for a particular group. Virtually all racial preferences designed to help blacks are permissible, according to this view, because they're not based on stigmatizing prejudice for whites, but instead on a desire to remedy the effects of discrimination in society as a whole. The weakness of this theory is obvious enough: not every form of discrimination is based on contempt or loathing. On the contrary, as Ruth Bader Ginsburg has argued, discrimination against women has long been rooted in the paternalistic idea that women need special and benevolent protection. And plenty of economic data suggest that most racial discrimination today is motivated not by hatred but by the administrative efficiency of generalizing from the average performance of a group to the likely performance of one of its members.

Instead of siding with either the liberal or conservative theories of affirmative action, Powell tried to mix and match them in cases after *Bakke*. Borrowing the individual responsibility position from the conservatives, Powell said institutions could engage in affirmative action only if they themselves had been guilty of discrimination. And borrowing the group oppression position from the liberals, Powell said the minorities could benefit from affirmative action even if they themselves had not been victims of discrimination.

The Texas case shows the illogic of this compromise. It's beyond dispute that the University of Texas discriminated notoriously against blacks in the past. But 1994 is not 1946; and the law school that rejected Cheryl Hopwood is a very different place than the law school that rejected Heman Sweatt. And despite the historical record, Judge Sparks's efforts to link the beneficiaries of Texas's current racial preferences with the victims of Texas's past racial discrimination seem particularly strained. He emphasizes, for example, that the parents of black applicants to the University of Texas today were discriminated against by the state of Texas a generation ago. This local discrimination, he suggests, may account for the persistent gaps between the scores of white and black applicants to the university. But the argument falters on an inconvenient fact: Texas admits most of its black law students from the pool of out-of-state applicants, who can hardly claim to have been handicapped by the legacy of discrimination in Texas. The existence of a national applicant pool tends to undermine any claims that the university is engaging in geographically precise compensation for its sins.

The *Hopwood* case, in short, exposes the implausible and increasingly esoteric foundations on which the law of affirmative action now rests. To accept the intellectual framework of *Bakke*, you have to accept a series of premises that are hard to reconcile with the cold data: that race can be a plus factor rather than a decisive factor in admissions decisions; that the need for racial preferences will soon disappear; and, most exotically of all, that institutions that have discriminated in the past can atone for their sins by projecting the effects of their discrimination into the future. Whatever its value as an act of public relations, Justice Powell's opinion in *Bakke* clearly has failed as an act of constitutional interpretation.

If the Court chooses to use the *Hopwood* case as an opportunity to re-examine *Bakke* in the next few years, there is a more convincing theory. As Andrew Kull argues in *The Colorblind Constitution*, the framers of the 14th Amendment did not intend to forbid all racial preferences, but only those that were unreasonable or unrelated to legitimate public purposes. They were especially concerned about laws like the Black Codes that extended unequal punishments, and unequal benefits, to blacks and whites. For better or for worse, therefore, fidelity to constitutional history supports, rather than undermines, the notion that the Supreme Court should pick and choose among racial classifications, upholding the reasonable ones and striking down the unreasonable ones. And in trying to refine the vague standard of reasonableness, the Court might indeed focus on whether the burdens of a racial classification are focused unfairly on particular individuals.

This weak colorblind principle would probably permit racial preferences along the Texas model, in college and graduate school admissions, because their burdens fall on a wide and diffuse group. Between the ninety-fourth percentile, which is the median for white applicants, and the eighty-ninth percentile, which is the median for black applicants, the University of Texas has to pass over one thousand whites for every black applicant that it admits. The disappointment of the rejected whites should not be minimized; but law schools, like undergraduate colleges, have never pretended to cultivate academic distinction alone: they seek to train not only legal scholars but also politicians and local worthies.

Moreover, unlike the highly qualified Alan Bakke, who clearly would have been admitted to the University of California in a colorblind world, the University of Texas refused to concede that the four plaintiffs in the *Hopwood* case would have been admitted on the merits. All four had adequate but unexceptional academic records that put them squarely in the broad middle range of the Texas applicant pool; and most were admitted to less prestigious law schools. Since Texas has to reject hundreds of applicants like Cheryl Hopwood, it's hard to argue that she is being singled out unfairly to bear the full weight of the racial preferences. Perhaps a more qualified plaintiff could have argued more convincingly that her expectations were frustrated.

Once racial preferences are extended beyond college and graduate school admissions, however, the burdens become far less diffuse. Consider the case of faculty hiring. The number of positions are far more limited; and when a certain number of them are set aside only for blacks, there are especially heavy costs on the rejected whites, who have invested an extraordinary amount of time in specialized preparation and are likely to have many fewer alternatives than students applying to graduate schools. There also seems far less justification for using group membership as a stand-in for intellectual diversity than in student admissions, where the actual views of applicants are hard to discern. And while even mediocre law students may go on to be successful lawyers or politicians, the standards for scholarly success are far more precise and objective. All this suggests that the "faculty diversity" argument that Deval Patrick is pressing in the New Jersey case is constitutionally as well as educationally questionable.

As the over-reaching of Patrick demonstrates, the Supreme Court's careful distinctions between permissible and impermissible affirmative action are being eroded or ignored in the wake of the political impulse to achieve proportionate racial representation in every sub-department of society. This impulse, which comes perilously close to discrimination for its own sake, refuses to engage the real question in the affirmative action debate—namely, what are the *justifications* for favoring members of one race over another in very different spheres and contexts? The only hope of avoiding a descent into pure racialism is to admit candidly that racial preferences have costs, and to set precise and legally enforceable boundaries. That project, thankfully, has now begun.

III. THE UNIVERSITY AND THE WORKPLACE

Editor's Introduction

Central to the conflict over affirmative action is the issue of reverse discrimination, which has created a new species of victim, the white male. In the opening article of Section Three, Christopher Shea, writing in *The Chronicle of Higher Education*, focuses upon UCLA's admissions system in which race is a strong factor. Shea adds, however, that, "unassisted," very few of the African American or Latino students who applied could meet admissions standards; and a system was accordingly devised to get them into the school. UCLA admits 60 percent of its class from applicants with the highest academic rankings—largely white and Asian American. Another committee ranks the remaining applicants on "supplemental" qualities that include race and family background as well as academic achievement; of these many who are given preference are African- or Mexican-American. Thus, 40 percent of the students in UCLA are admitted through a special program. If affirmative action were to be eliminated, the proportion of black students would fall from 7 percent to something like 1 or 2 percent. If affirmative action were changed to emphasize economic status rather than race, the university's dilemma would not disappear because there would be greater numbers of disadvantaged whites to consider, so the percentage of minority students would still be diminished to minuscule proportions. Although there are inequities in the present system, Shea notes, no other arrangement offers a greater prospect of fairness to all.

Reverse discrimination is the subject of an article by Robin Wilson, also writing in *The Chronicle of Higher Education*. At Northwestern University, Wilson notes, white male graduate students are likely to be confronted by a difficult dilemma. While they are likely to endorse affirmative action in principle, they are also aware that this very policy will make it difficult for them to be hired in academia, where jobs are scarce and are likely to be allocated to women and minorities. Reverse discrimination is the issue in an article from *The Atlantic Monthly* by Stanley Fish. Fish begins by asking whether special privileges claimed by blacks and

84

denied to whites are not just as bad as special privileges that had been claimed by whites and denied to blacks. In the course of a strongly reasoned argument, he concludes that they are not equivalent; that in ways both glaring and subtle, blacks have been denied a level playing field in the contest of life.

Next, a staff written article in *The Economist*, points out that even if affirmative action is overruled in the courts, the corporate community will almost certainly continue to make voluntary efforts of its own in that direction. Most of the biggest firms in America have "diversity programs" in place, and recognize the advantages of a diverse workforce in a multicultural society.

In a following article in *Forbes*, Nina Munk comments on the problems with set-aside contracts for favored minority businesses. According to a U.S. Supreme Court ruling in 1989, set-asides are unconstitutional unless a significant disparity can be shown between the number of minority contractors ready and able to perform work for a municipality and the number actually engaged; and it must further be shown that the disparity was caused by intentional discrimination (something not easy to prove). The issue of disparity has become so complicated that organizations specializing in "disparity studies" have sprung up and are flourishing. Complicating matters further are the growing lists of minorities claiming eligibility. It seems to Munk that the minority set-asides are a modern-day equivalent of old-fashioned political patronage. Finally, Catherine Yang in an article from *BusinessWeek* shows that although set-aside programs can be abused (particularly when minority companies are really a "front" for white contractors) they also have their success stories in which minority companies have received an initial hand-up and then thrived on their own.

UNDER UCLA'S ELABORATE SYSTEM
RACE MAKES A BIG DIFFERENCE[1]

Both critics and supporters of affirmative action think they can prove their cases by pointing to the University of California at Los Angeles.

One side says the admissions system, which produced a freshman class this year that is less than one-third white, reveals an obsession with ethnicity. The other side says that UCLA has seamlessly united its commitments to diversity and to academic merit.

As state legislators and regents debate racial preferences, UCLA's chancellor, Charles E. Young, has invited even more scrutiny. He has called for candor about the weight given to race in admissions, arguing that opposition to affirmative action is founded on misconceptions. "We won't convince everyone we're right," he says, "but some may say, 'What they're doing isn't as bad as we thought.'"

Some here remain reticent about discussing differences in the academic qualifications of various ethnic groups. Still, by looking at information from three of the university's schools—the College of Letters and Science, the law school, and the medical school—it's possible to get a sense of how often race makes the difference.

The college and the law school fill nearly two-thirds of their slots by ignoring race and looking for high grades and test scores. Overwhelmingly, the students in those slots are whites and Asian Americans. Almost all black and Latino students get in through a second route, in which the university takes race and family income into account.

Starting with Demographics

The programs that boost the admission rates of black and Latino students in the college and law school theoretically also help

---

[1]Article by Christopher Shea, senior editor, from *The Chronicle of Higher Education* 41:A12-4 Ap 28 '95. Copyright © 1995 by *The Chronicle of Higher Education*. Reprinted by permission.

poor white and Asian-American students, as does a special admissions subcommittee in the medical school. But compared to the number of students who get help because of race, few such students are admitted.

For the College of Letters and Science, the argument for affirmative action begins with demographics. In the state's system of higher education, the nine University of California campuses are open to high school graduates with averages of B+ or better; they make up the top 12.5 percent of their class. Students with lower grades are eligible if they do well on the Scholastic Assessment Test (SAT).

What makes diversity a challenge is that so few black and Latino students are even in the running for admission. Only about 5 percent of black high school graduates, and 4 percent of Latino students, meet the minimum requirements. In contrast, 13 percent of whites and 32 percent of the state's Asian Americans meet the criteria.

So while there are roughly 7 times as many white students as black students in the state, there are more than 15 times as many eligible white students as eligible black students. Most years, there have been fewer than one thousand black high school seniors in the entire state qualified for admission to the U.C. system.

UCLA's applicant pool—20,100 students in 1994—is similarly dominated by qualified white and Asian students. To bring the proportions closer to those of the state's population, the university has struck a balance between merit and diversity.

Applications Are Ranked

After a student's application arrives at the college, it is read by two staff members and given a rank of one to six. Students with one's and two's, the highest marks, tend to have straight-A averages. UCLA gets 60 percent of its class by admitting the students with the highest academic rankings.

Of 6,801 students admitted to UCLA last year [1995] on strictly academic grounds, 1.1 percent were black and 4.7 percent were Latino. Forty percent were white, and nearly 48 percent were Asian American.

Both administrators and students say those numbers are in large part a measure of racial disparities in wealth and educational opportunities. "Chicano and African-American students don't live in places where you can go to a course to prepare for the SAT," says Dorene Martínez, a freshman involved in the Latino student group Mecha.

Her father is a construction worker and her mother a clerk at a hospital, but she argues that she and other Latino students had disadvantages that white middle-class kids did not. "It's not just money," she says. "It's about pride, about knowing you can be educated and that you have potential."

Her friend, sophomore Briseyda Fernandez Zárate, grew up in a farming community in central California, where both of her parents are grape harvesters, and her high school offered only one Advanced Placement course. "I had the potential but not the opportunity," she says.

At the same time the academic rankings are being done, another committee ranks students on the same one-to-six scale for "supplemental" qualities, including race and family background.

Combining the Two Scores

In this ranking, race is a big factor: All black and Mexican-American students from California get a one or two. White and Asian students are ranked on a broader scale, of one to five. (Sixes are reserved for out-of-state residents.) Getting a one or a two on this scale does not insure admission the way a one or a two on the academic scale does, but it guarantees that an applicant will be considered, even if he or she just barely meets UCLA's requirements.

The other 40 percent of the students in the college are admitted through a combination of the two scores. Rae Lee Siporin, the director of undergraduate admissions, says racial diversity is not the only reason for looking beyond grades. Emphasizing grades alone, she says, would produce a bland class. "We get over 8,000 applicants with a 4.0 GPA. I don't think we can afford to accept only students who have a 4.0."

Yet the chances are small that white or Asian students get in for any reason other than grades: 5 percent of the white students admitted to the freshman class in 1994 got in via the second tier of admissions, as did 17 percent of Asian Americans. On the other hand, 88 percent of black students were admitted that way, and 83 percent of Latino students.

All of them have at least B+ averages, but critics say the dual admission system still creates two groups with very different abilities. Black students' average SAT score, 951, is far below that of whites (1,186) or Asians (1,182). The admissions staff discounts SAT comparisons because black students lag behind whites nationally on the test, but the 235-point gap at UCLA is even wider than the 198-point national gap. There is a gap in high school GPA's as well: 3.5 for black students, just about 4.0 for whites, including extra weight for honors classes.

Graduation rates are also used to make this point. In the 1990s, the graduation rate for black students has been about 52 percent, and for Latino students 60 percent. The comparable figures for white students and Asian students have been 80 percent and 77 percent.

Chancellor Young, however, notes that the gap has been closing for the past five years, and that UCLA's graduation rates for black and Latino students are better than those of most other public colleges in the country.

Like the College of Letters and Science, the law school relies partly on a formula. Each student's GPA and test scores are converted to a numerical scale, and the school fills 60 percent of its class by admitting students above a certain cutoff point.

Students admitted this way are even more homogeneous than those admitted by the undergraduate college's academics review, says Michael D. Rappaport, the law school's dean of admissions. The law school received 5,072 applications for the 337 spots in the 1994–95 first-year class. Of those students, 749 were admitted on academics alone, among whom 585 were white, 140 Asian American, 19 Latino, 3 black, and 2 American Indian. In terms of diversity, the story gets worse: All three black students turned down UCLA for other law schools.

Reviews by Student Groups

Given California's ethnic makeup, administrators call that mix unthinkable. "Do you think in this day and age we would be justified—legally or morally—if we had the only public law school in the country without any black students?" asks Mr. Rappaport.

He acknowledges that race is a "major factor" in rounding out the class. Even student groups representing blacks, Hispanics, and Asians are given some say. They receive copies of applications and can offer their own lists of the strongest candidates. White applicants do not receive such reviews.

"We look for signs that people have overcome obstacles," says Kathay Feng, president of the Asian-student group. "We don't say, 'This person is Asian and so should be recommended.'"

Jack Schaedel, executive director of the Republican Law Students Association, opposes all racial preferences and believes that they are least defensible in professional schools. "At a law school, every person, black or white, is coming out of a good four-year college," he says. "At some point everyone should compete on an even playing field."

Reviews Dropped at Michigan

The University of Michigan's law school stopped letting minority students review applications from students of the same race in 1992, worried that the Education Department was preparing to investigate its system for possible bias. Mr. Rappaport says that the student groups here do no more than write additional letters of recommendation, so he has no doubt the law school's admissions system is proper.

The medical school has an admissions subcommittee that reviews applicants claiming disadvantage because of race or poverty. Although the Education Department has been critical of separate committees that review applications from minority students, the medical school says its system presents no problem because the subcommittee considers disadvantaged students of any ethnicity.

The subcommittee, made up of thirty professors and five students, does not make admissions decisions. It reviews the applications of students who have been interviewed and passes along its ranking of them to an executive admissions committee. In 1994, the medical school had 5,625 applicants for 121 spots, and about 750 students got interviews.

The medical school reported that 515 students who requested special consideration because of racial or economic disadvantage were Asian American, 351 were black, 296 were Mexican American, 241 were white, 133 were Hispanic, and 32 were Puerto Rican.

It is rare, however, for a white or Asian-American student to be admitted from that category. Out of 62 students admitted that way, 56 were black or Mexican American.

Martin A. Pops, the school's associate dean for student affairs, says eliminating affirmative action "wouldn't make any difference at all" to admissions at the medical school, because the system doesn't use formulas to raise the proportion of minority students. But officials in the College of Letters and Science and in the law school argue that it would make all the difference in the world in their schools. The college's admissions committee estimates that the proportion of black students in its freshman class of 3,600 would drop from 7 percent to 1 or 2 percent under an academics-only system, and that the proportion of Latinos would plummet from 19 percent to below 10 percent.

UCLA officials say that changing affirmative action to emphasize economic status rather than race—as many in the national debate suggest—would also diminish the number of minority students.

"There are an awful lot more white people in the country, a lot of whom can claim socio-economic disadvantage," says the law school's Mr. Rappaport. "It would dilute the pool."

A Drop in the Bucket

Without racial preferences, say educators here, the only path to admitting reasonable numbers of minority students would be massive investment in the inner city schools that serve many of them. Since the late 1970s, the college has offered academic counseling and SAT preparation courses in Los Angeles public schools, helping students become eligible for admission. But these efforts amount to "a drop in the bucket," says Ms. Siporin, the director of admissions.

The law school started its affirmative-action program in 1967 because no black students were making the cut on grades alone, a situation the university interpreted as racism's legacy. In 1995, says Mr. Rappaport, it's still the case that few blacks or Latinos would get in on grades alone, and he thinks that makes a continuing commitment to affirmative action an imperative.

"Is it fair?" he asks. "It's necessary. I'll put it that way."

AMONG WHITE MALES, JOKES AND ANECDOTES[2]

John Bishop begins a conversation about affirmative action by telling you he's in favor of it. He is quick to say he has "never felt there was anything unfair" about hiring preferences for women and members of racial minority groups.

But like other white men studying for their Ph.D.'s in English at Northwestern University, Mr. Bishop changes his outlook when you ask how affirmative action will affect *him*. "It's an accepted thing that people think, 'Oh, boy, if I were only a Caribbean lesbian doing post-colonial studies, I'd have a lot easier time getting a job,'" says Mr. Bishop, who will start looking for a teaching post . . . .

William J. Savage, Jr., finished his Ph.D. in English at Northwestern in 1992 and has yet to receive a teaching offer. He, too, tries to reconcile his support of affirmative action with his belief that it may be hurting him in the job market. "Speaking as a straight white male, I think affirmative action is a good thing," he says. But he can't overlook the facts: He has applied for almost three hundred jobs since he graduated and has received barely a nibble.

"It's become a family joke," he says. "You know, 'You're the wrong color, Bill. You can't get a job.'" Universities that may have passed over him because of his skin color have made a mistake, he says. "I'm an Irish working-class kid from a mean neighborhood of Chicago, and I would diversify the hell out of a department. But if all that matters is race and gender—which is all that matters now—I'm not going to get a job."

Seen as a Scapegoat

Conventional wisdom says that white men are bitter about losing jobs to women and blacks and are leading the charge to dismantle affirmative action. But conversations here with a group of white men who have their sights set on the professoriate reveal

[2]Article by Robin Wilson, senior writer, from *The Chronicle of Higher Education* 41:A20-1 Ap 28 '95. Copyright © 1995 by *The Chronicle of Higher Education*. Reprinted with permission.

that, for them, the issues are more complicated. Many of the nineteen white men studying graduate English at Northwestern are concerned that affirmative action becomes the scapegoat when white men don't get jobs. In reality, they say, the academic job market is so dismal these days that almost no one, regardless of gender or race, is finding work.

The students here pass around stories about universities that have received five hundred applications for a single teaching job. They'll tell you that only one of the five people who received doctorates in English from Northwestern last year [1994] has a full-time teaching job so far. That's not unusual these days, even for graduates of prestigious institutions like this one. "If people are angry about the job market, they say, 'Let's make it an issue of race,' rather than saying, 'This is a structural problem,'" says another of the Ph.D. candidates, Jon R. Neulieb. "Whenever there are issues of scarcity, people start looking for things to blame."

Brad Deane, who is studying Victorian literature, blames white men, not women or blacks. He says young people like himself are being shut out of academe by white men well beyond their prime who won't retire—and don't have to, because Congress has abolished mandatory retirement. He also points a finger at state legislatures, made up primarily of white men, which have cut money for higher education and have prompted universities to fill teaching slots with part-time workers rather than with tenure-track professors.

Still, the jokes and stories these men tell over beer at an Irish pub near the campus show they worry about whether their gender and their race are the real issues. "Next on Donahue: White male transsexuals who change their sex to get jobs," jokes one student. Says another: "A black lesbian with a nose ring studying literature by the disabled—that would get you a job." In fact, most affirmative-action policies do not cover gay men or lesbians. Even so, these students suspect that anyone who is not a straight white male has an advantage.

People Would Look Crestfallen

The problem with the jokes is that some of them mirror what has happened in real life. One story about a white woman who graduated from Northwestern in 1992 with a dissertation on African-American writers has become legendary. It is cited as evidence of how unfriendly the academy can be to white Ph.D.'s, even those who study hot topics.

The woman, Traci Carroll, traveled to three annual meetings of the Modern Language Association from 1992 to 1994 and had interviews with forty-one institutions. Only one called her back for a second interview. Ms. Carroll now has a three-year teaching post at that institution, Rhodes College. She believes that search committees thought she was black—because of her dissertation topic—and were uninterested in her once they learned she was not.

"People would look crestfallen when they saw I was white, and the conversation took on a perfunctory character," she says. "It is difficult enough to do your work without having to fight these other battles." She is considering leaving the field to become a massage therapist.

Ms. Carroll's experience worries the men who have gathered at Tommy Nevin's, the pub. They say affirmative action has influenced what is taught in the classroom. Anything multicultural, including black writers and gender studies, is hot these days. But white men can damage their career prospects by paying too much attention to such topics, they say.

Clay Cerny's dissertation on American literature and race after the Civil War includes four chapters on black writers. He is beginning to look for jobs that would require him to teach African-American literature. "I knew from the start that it might be harder for me because schools would be looking to put in my place minority scholars," he says. One person who interviewed him for a job asked him how he would respond to questions from black students who wondered why he was teaching African-American writing.

"What I tell myself," he says, "is that sooner or later, I'm going to find a diverse department where I fit in as a white male."

You're Going To Have To Do More

Josh Charlson went to a discussion about the job market recently and asked the professor who was speaking whether someone who was completing a dissertation in American literature would be more likely to get a job if he covered African-American writers. The speaker said Yes. The topic doesn't fit into Mr. Charlson's dissertation, so he plans to try to make himself more

marketable by publishing an article on African-American literature, "to fill in the gaps," he says.

Some white men at Northwestern have already been told that
their sex and race are problems, regardless of what their dissertation covers. Todd Trubey says when he applied for a temporary
teaching position, someone at the institution told him that his credentials were good, but that the college was looking to hire a
woman or a member of a minority group. Many of the men here
have been told that they need to do topnotch work if they want
even to be considered for jobs.

"A senior woman in our department told me, 'You are a white
male, so you're going to have to do more,'" says Joe Kraus, who
is in his third year of studying 20th-century American and ethnic-
immigrant writers. "She said, 'You've got two strikes against you,
so you'd better be very good.'"

Mr. Savage, the graduate who has applied for nearly three
hundred jobs, thinks he is good, but he is not sure that is the issue.
"I am willing to accept the fact that I am the one paying for white-
male badness of the past, and I might never be anything but a
bartender," he says. But. he adds, "I'd like to be able to get a job
and pay my student loans off and be able to go to the dentist once
in a while."

REVERSE RACISM, OR HOW THE POT GOT TO CALL THE KETTLE BLACK[3]

*In America "whites once set themselves apart from blacks and claimed
privileges for themselves while denying them to others," the author writes.
"Now, on the basis of race, blacks are claiming special status and reserving
for themselves privileges they deny to others. Isn't one as bad as the other?
The answer is no."*

I take my text from George Bush, who, in an address to the
United Nations on September 23, 1991, said this of the UN reso-

[3]Article by Stanley Fish, professor of english and of law at Duke University,
from *The Atlantic Monthly* 272:128-36 N '93. Copyright © 1993 by Stanley Fish. Reprinted with permission.

lution equating Zionism with racism: "Zionism . . . is the idea
that led to the creation of a home for the Jewish people. . . . And
to equate Zionism with the intolerable sin of racism is to twist history and forget the terrible plight of Jews in World War II and
indeed throughout history." What happened in World War II was
that six million Jews were exterminated by people who regarded
them as racially inferior and a danger to Aryan purity. What happened after World War II was that the survivors of that Holo-
caust established a Jewish state—that is, a state centered on
Jewish history, Jewish values, and Jewish traditions: in short, a Je-
wocentric state. What President Bush objected to was the logical
sleight of hand by which these two actions were declared equivalent because they were both expressions of racial exclusiveness.
Ignored, as Bush said, was the *historical* difference between
them—the difference between a program of genocide and the
determination of those who escaped it to establish a community
in which they would be the makers, not the victims, of the laws.

Only if racism is thought of as something that occurs principally in the mind, a falling-away from proper notions of universal
equality, can the desire of a victimized and terrorized people to
band together be declared morally identical to the actions of their
would-be executioners. Only when the actions of the two groups
are detached from the historical conditions of their emergence
and given a purely abstract description can they be made inter-
changeable. Bush was saying to the United Nations, "Look, the
Nazis' conviction of racial superiority generated a policy of sys-
tematic genocide; the Jews' experience of centuries of persecution in almost every country on earth generated a desire for a
homeland of their own. If you manage somehow to convince
yourself that these are the same, it is you, not the Zionists, who
are morally confused, and the reason you are morally confused
is that you have forgotten history."

A Key Distinction

What I want to say, following Bush's reasoning, is that a similar forgetting of history has in recent years allowed some people
to argue, and argue persuasively, that affirmative action is reverse racism. The very phrase "reverse racism" contains the argument in exactly the form to which Bush objected: In this country
whites once set themselves apart from blacks and claimed privi-

leges for themselves while denying them to others. Now, on the basis of race, blacks are claiming special status and reserving for themselves privileges they deny to others. Isn't one as bad as the other? The answer is no. One can see why by imagining that it is . . . 1955, and that we are in a town in the South with two more or less distinct communities, one white and one black. No doubt each community would have a ready store of dismissive epithets, ridiculing stories, self-serving folk myths, and expressions of plain hatred, all directed at the other community, and all based in racial hostility. Yet to regard their respective racisms—if that is the word—as equivalent would be bizarre, for the hostility of one group stems not from any wrong done to it but from its wish to protect its ability to deprive citizens of their voting rights, to limit access to educational institutions, to prevent entry into the economy except at the lowest and most menial levels, and to force members of the stigmatized group to ride in the back of the bus. The hostility of the other group is the result of these actions, and whereas hostility and racial anger are unhappy facts wherever they are found, a distinction must surely be made between the ideological hostility of the oppressors and the experience-based hostility of those who have been oppressed.

Not to make that distinction is, adapting George Bush's words, to twist history and forget the terrible plight of African-Americans in the more than two hundred years of this country's existence. Moreover, to equate the efforts to remedy that plight with the actions that produced it is to twist history even further. Those efforts, designed to redress the imbalances caused by long-standing discrimination, are called affirmative action; to argue that affirmative action, which gives preferential treatment to disadvantaged minorities as part of a plan to achieve social equality, is no different from the policies that created the disadvantages in the first place is a travesty of reasoning. "Reverse racism" is a cogent description of affirmative action only if one considers the cancer of racism to be morally and medically indistinguishable from the therapy we apply to it. A cancer is an invasion of the body's equilibrium, and so is chemotherapy; but we do not decline to fight the disease because the medicine we employ is also disruptive of normal functioning. Strong illness, strong remedy: the formula is as appropriate to the health of the body politic as it is to that of the body proper.

At this point someone will always say, "But two wrongs don't make a right; if it was wrong to treat blacks unfairly, it is wrong to give blacks preference and thereby treat whites unfairly." This objection is just another version of the forgetting and rewriting of history. The work is done by the adverb "unfairly," which suggests two more or less equal parties, one of whom has been unjustly penalized by an incompetent umpire. But blacks have not simply been treated unfairly; they have been subjected first to decades of slavery, and then to decades of second-class citizenship, widespread legalized discrimination, economic persecution, educational deprivation, and cultural stigmatization. They have been bought, sold, killed, beaten, raped, excluded, exploited, shamed, and scorned for a very long time. The word "unfair" is hardly an adequate description of their experience, and the belated gift of "fairness" in the form of a resolution no longer to discriminate against them legally is hardly an adequate remedy for the deep disadvantages that the prior discrimination has produced. When the deck is stacked against you in more ways than you can even count, it is small consolation to hear that you are now free to enter the game and take your chances.

A Tilted Field

The same insincerity and hollowness of promise infect another formula that is popular with the anti-affirmative-action crowd: the formula of the level playing field. Here the argument usually takes the form of saying "It is undemocratic to give one class of citizens advantages at the expense of other citizens; the truly democratic way is to have a level playing field to which everyone has access and where everyone has a fair and equal chance to succeed on the basis of his or her merit." Fine words—but they conceal the facts of the situation as it has been given to us by history: the playing field is already tilted in favor of those by whom and for whom it was constructed in the first place. If mastery of the requirements for entry depends upon immersion in the cultural experiences of the mainstream majority, if the skills that make for success are nurtured by institutions and cultural practices from which the disadvantaged minority has been systematically excluded, if the language and ways of comporting oneself that identify a player as "one of us" are alien to the lives minorities are forced to live, then words like "fair" and "equal" are cruel jokes, for what they promote and celebrate is an institutionalized unfairness and a perpetuated inequality. The playing field is already tilted, and the resistance to altering it by the mechanisms of affirmative action is in fact a determination to make sure that the present imbalances persist as long as possible.

One way of tilting the field is the Scholastic Aptitude Test (SAT). This test figures prominently in Dinesh D'Souza's book *Illiberal Education* (1991), in which one finds many examples of white or Asian students denied admission to colleges and universities even though their SAT scores were higher than the scores of some others—often African Americans—who were admitted to the same institution. This, D'Souza says, is evidence that as a result of affirmative-action policies colleges and universities tend "to depreciate the importance of merit criteria in admissions." D'Souza's assumption—and it is one that many would share—is that the test does in fact measure *merit*, with merit understood as a quality objectively determined in the same way that body temperature can be objectively determined.

In fact, however, the test is nothing of the kind. Statistical studies have suggested that test scores reflect income and socioeconomic status. It has been demonstrated again and again that scores vary in relation to cultural background; the test's questions assume a certain uniformity in educational experience and lifestyle and penalize those who, for whatever reason, have had a different experience and lived different kinds of lives. In short, what is being measured by the SAT is not absolutes like native ability and merit but accidents like birth, social position, access to libraries, and the opportunity to take vacations or to take SAT prep courses.

Furthermore, as David Owen notes in *None of the Above: Behind the Myth of Scholastic Aptitude* (1985), the "correlation between SAT scores and college grades . . . is lower than the correlation between weight and height; in other words you would have a better chance of predicting a person's height by looking at his weight than you would of predicting his freshman grades by looking only at his SAT scores." Everywhere you look in the SAT story, the claims of fairness, objectivity, and neutrality fall away, to be replaced by suspicions of specialized measures and unfair advantages.

Against this background a point that in isolation might have a questionable force takes on a special and even explanatory resonance: the principal deviser of the test was an out-and-out racist. In 1923 Carl Campbell Brigham published a book called *A Study of American Intelligence*, in which, as Owen notes, he declared, among other things, that we faced in America "a possibility of racial admixture . . . infinitely worse than that faced by any European country today, for we are incorporating the Negro into our racial stock, while all of Europe is comparatively free of this taint." Brigham had earlier analyzed the Army Mental Tests using classifications drawn from another racist text, Madison Grant's *The Passing of the Great Race*, which divided American society into four distinct racial strains, with Nordic, blue-eyed, blond people at the pinnacle and the American Negro at the bottom. Nevertheless, in 1925 Brigham became a director of testing for the College Board, and developed the SAT. So here is the great SAT test, devised by a racist in order to confirm racist assumptions, measuring not native ability but cultural advantage, an uncertain indicator of performance, an indicator of very little except what money and social privilege can buy. And it is in the name of this mechanism that we are asked to reject affirmative action and reaffirm "the importance of merit criteria in admissions."

The Reality of Discrimination

Nevertheless, there is at least one more card to play against affirmative action, and it is a strong one. Granted that the playing field is not level and that access to it is reserved for an already advantaged elite, the disadvantages suffered by others are less racial—at least in 1993—than socioeconomic. Therefore shouldn't, as D'Souza urges, "universities . . . retain their policies of preferential treatment, but alter their criteria of application from race to socioeconomic disadvantage," and thus avoid the unfairness of current policies that reward middle-class or affluent blacks at the expense of poor whites? One answer to this question is given by D'Souza himself when he acknowledges that the overlap between minority groups and the poor is very large—a point underscored by the former Secretary of Education Lamar Alexander, who said, in response to a question about funds targeted for black students, "Ninety-eight percent of race-specific scholarships do not involve constitutional problems." He meant, I take it, that 98 percent of race-specific scholarships were also scholarships to the economically disadvantaged.

Still, the other two percent—nonpoor, middle-class, economically favored blacks—are receiving special attention on the basis of disadvantages they do not experience. What about them? The force of the question depends on the assumption that in this day and age race could not possibly be a serious disadvantage to those who are otherwise well positioned in the society. But the lie was given dramatically to this assumption in a 1991 broadcast of the ABC program *Prime Time Live*. In a stunning fifteen-minute segment reporters and a camera crew followed two young men of equal education, cultural sophistication, level of apparent affluence, and so forth around St. Louis, a city where neither was known. The two differed in only a single respect: one was white, the other black. But that small difference turned out to mean everything. In a series of encounters with shoe salesmen, record-store employees, rental agents, landlords, employment agencies, taxicab drivers, and ordinary citizens, the black member of the pair was either ignored or given a special and suspicious attention. He was asked to pay more for the same goods or come up with a larger down payment for the same car, was turned away as a prospective tenant, was rejected as a prospective taxicab fare, was treated with contempt and irritation by clerks and bureaucrats, and in every way possible was made to feel inferior and unwanted.

The inescapable conclusion was that alike though they may have been in almost all respects, one of these young men, because he was black, would lead a significantly lesser life than his white counterpart: he would be housed less well and at greater expense; he would pay more for services and products when and if he was given the opportunity to buy them; he would have difficulty establishing credit; the first emotions he would inspire on the part of many people he met would be distrust and fear; his abilities would be discounted even before he had a chance to display them; and, above all, the treatment he received from minute to minute would chip away at his self-esteem and self-confidence with consequences that most of us could not even imagine. As the young man in question said at the conclusion of the broadcast, "You walk down the street with a suit and tie and it doesn't matter. Someone will make determinations about you, determinations that affect the quality of your life."

Of course, the same determinations are being made quite early on by kindergarten teachers, grade school principals, high school guidance counselors, and the like, with results that cut across socioeconomic lines and place young black men and women in the ranks of the disadvantaged no matter what the bank accounts of their parents happen to show. Racism is a cultural fact, and although its effects may to some extent be diminished by socioeconomic variables, those effects will still be sufficiently great to warrant the nation's attention and thus the continuation of affirmative-action policies. This is true even of the field thought to be dominated by blacks and often cited as evidence of the equal opportunities society now affords them. I refer, of course, to professional athletics. But national self-congratulation on this score might pause in the face of a few facts: A minuscule number of African Americans ever receive a paycheck from a professional team. Even though nearly 1,600 daily newspapers report on the exploits of black athletes, they employ only seven full-time black sports columnists. Despite repeated pledges and resolutions, major-league teams have managed to put only a handful of blacks and Hispanics in executive positions.

Why Me?

When all is said and done, however, one objection to affirmative action is unanswerable on its own terms, and that is the objection of the individual who says, "Why me? Sure, discrimination has persisted for many years, and I acknowledge that the damage done has not been removed by changes in the law. But why me? I didn't own slaves; I didn't vote to keep people on the back of the bus; I didn't turn water hoses on civil-rights marchers. Why, then, should I be the one who doesn't get the job or who doesn't get the scholarship or who gets bumped back to the waiting list?"

I sympathize with this feeling, if only because in a small way I have had the experience that produces it. I was recently nominated for an administrative post at a large university. Early signs were encouraging, but after an interval I received official notice that I would not be included at the next level of consideration, and subsequently I was told unofficially that at some point a decision had been made to look only in the direction of women and minorities. Although I was disappointed, I did not conclude that the situation was "unfair," because the policy was obviously not directed at me—at no point in the proceedings did someone say, "Let's find a way to rule out Stanley Fish." Nor was it directed even at persons of my race and sex—the policy was not intended to disenfranchise white males. Rather, the policy was driven by other considerations, and it was only as a by-product of those considerations—not as the main goal—that white males like me were rejected. Given that the institution in question has a high percentage of minority students, a very low percentage of minority faculty, and an even lower percentage of minority administrators, it made perfect sense to focus on women and minority candidates, and within that sense, not as the result of prejudice, my whiteness and maleness became disqualifications.

I can hear the objection in advance: "What's the difference? Unfair is unfair: you didn't get the job; you didn't even get on the short list." The difference is not in the outcome but in the ways of thinking that led up to the outcome. It is the difference between an unfairness that befalls one as the unintended effect of a policy rationally conceived and an unfairness that is pursued as an end in itself. It is the difference between the awful unfairness of Nazi extermination camps and the unfairness to Palestinian Arabs that arose from, but was not the chief purpose of, the founding of a Jewish state.

The New Bigotry

The point is not a difficult one, but it is difficult to see when the unfairness scenarios are presented as simple contrasts between two decontextualized persons who emerge from nowhere to contend for a job or a place in a freshman class. Here is student A; he has a board score of 1,300. And here is student B; her board score is only 1,200, yet she is admitted and A is rejected. Is that fair? Given the minimal information provided, the answer is of course no. But if we expand our horizons and consider fairness in relation to the cultural and institutional histories that have brought the two students to this point, histories that weigh on them even if they are not the histories' authors, then both the question and the answer suddenly grow more complicated.

The sleight-of-hand logic that first abstracts events from history and then assesses them from behind a veil of willed ignorance gains some of its plausibility from another key word in the anti-affirmative-action lexicon. That word is "individual," as in "The American way is to focus on the rights of individuals rather than groups." Now, "individual" and "individualism" have been honorable words in the American political vocabulary, and they have often been well employed in the fight against various tyrannies. But like any other word or concept, individualism can be perverted to serve ends the opposite of those it originally served, and this is what has happened when in the name of individual rights, millions of individuals are enjoined from redressing historically documented wrongs. How is this managed? Largely in the same way that the invocation of fairness is used to legitimize an institutionalized inequality. First one says, in the most solemn of tones, that the protection of individual rights is the chief obligation of society. Then one defines individuals as souls sent into the world with equal entitlements as guaranteed either by their Creator or by the Constitution. Then one pretends that nothing has happened to them since they stepped onto the world's stage. And then one says of these carefully denatured souls that they will all be treated in the same way, irrespective of any of the differences that history has produced. Bizarre as it may seem, individualism in this argument turns out to mean that everyone is or should be the *same*. This dismissal of individual difference in the name of the individual would be funny were its consequences not so serious: it is the mechanism by which imbalances and inequities suffered by millions of people through no fault of their own can be sanitized and even celebrated as the natural workings of unfettered democracy.

"Individualism," "fairness," "merit"—these three words are continually misappropriated by bigots who have learned that they need not put on a white hood or bar access to the ballot box in order to secure their ends. Rather, they need only clothe themselves in a vocabulary plucked from its historical context and made into the justification for attitudes and policies they would not acknowledge if frankly named.

AFFIRMATIVE ACTION: A STRONG PREJUDICE[4]

When a district sales manager for Avon Products in Atlanta noticed an influx of Vietnamese and Korean families in 1993, she sniffed an opportunity. She quickly recruited Vietnamese and Korean staff to sell Avon cosmetics door-to-door, hoping that they would have the language skills and cultural know-how to sell to this mostly first- and second-generation population. The hunch proved right: the Asian-American Avon ladies cleaned up.

The story is not unusual. Although many politicians want to axe government affirmative-action programmes, much of corporate America has decided that having a diverse workforce can be a business asset. A recent study found that nearly three-quarters of the fifty biggest firms in America had "directors of diversity" or "diversity managers" whose job is to modify corporate culture so that it suits the needs of all employees. "Diversity training" is becoming *de rigueur* for managers in large companies. A diversity industry, charging fees as high as $10,000 a day, runs sessions on valuing differences, sexual harassment, "style diversity," and other such fads.

Why all the fuss? The answer lies in demographics. By [the year] 2000 the World Bank reckons white males will make up only 45 percent of America's workforce. Employers must therefore fish from a larger, more confusing talent pool than in the days when the man in the grey flannel suit was always white and middle-class. Personnel managers report that new job applicants are quick to ask about diversity policies. Having something to say in response has become a crucial recruiting ploy.

Thus Exxon offers internships for promising "minority" applicants; AT&T's mentoring programme focuses specifically on women and minorities. Amoco's chairman, Lawrence Fuller, heads the company's "diversity advisory council," which discusses company policy with employee representatives for women, blacks, Hispanics, and the disabled. Hewlett-Packard's chief executive, Lew Platt, plugs diversity as one of the company's top three priorities, along with customer satisfaction and order fulfilment.

[4]Article by staff writer, from *The Economist* 335:69–70 Je 17 '95. Copyright © 1995 by The Economist Newspaper Group, Inc. Reprinted with permission. Further reproduction prohibited.

Each of Gannett's eighty-three daily newspapers makes a self-assessment of progress in diversity that goes to the board of directors, itself a third female and a third non-white.

Generational change also plays a role. As the children of the feminist and civil-rights movements climb the corporate ladder, they bring their values with them. Madelyn Condit, a headhunter at Korn/Ferry International in Chicago, says that she has seen a dramatic increase in the desire to recruit—and poach—minority managers. "It's illegal to recruit a certain gender or ethnic group," she observes, "but maybe 70 percent of our customers would like to see women or minorities in the candidate pool. That was not the case five years ago." Ironically, part of the reason may be that personnel departments were long considered good places to use to meet affirmative-action targets; now that women and minorities have taken over these offices, they run the show.

The demographic forces that are changing the look of a big American company's workforce are also changing its customer base. The first to spot this were firms in consumer-products and services. Some 130 of Sears, Roebuck's 800 stores, for example, are in or near Hispanic neighborhoods; Sears now staffs these with Hispanic or bilingual employees. AT&T has built support among recent immigrants with its Language Line, which non-English speakers can call to get an AT&T translator—in 140 languages. Pillsbury and Kraft General Foods say that diversifying the ranks of management has helped them to develop markets for black and Hispanic-style foods.

Globalization, with all its cultural pitfalls, is also forcing American multinationals to reassess the value of their domestic workforce. Many large firms are searching for ABCs (American-born Chinese) to send to Hong Kong and China. Digital Equipment has asked an in-house black employee group to help crack the South African computer market. Electronic Data Systems (EDS), a Dallas-based computer-services company, recently hired a Japanese-American to head its Tokyo office; one of his tasks is to re-engineer the corporate style after an overly Texan debut. To help it crack the Asian market, NYNEX, a New York telecoms company, is encouraging American staff—particularly Chinese and Korean speakers—to take their talent to Asia for a time.

The Bottom Line

Is diversity just a fad? A 1993 survey by the Virginia-based Society for Human Resources Management found that fewer than a third of companies considered their diversity training efforts to be successful; half thought they made no difference. Critics are right when they say the "diversity hustle" can drift into excess. Diversity consultants have been known to provoke lawsuits, stir up ethnic tensions or humiliate white men. (One response: programmes on "white maleism.") Personnel departments are not averse to a spot of empire-building.

There is a hard-headed logic to the diversity trend, though, that suggests that it will endure. Only 4 percent of the executives in a 1994 Conference Board survey gave "social responsibility" as the reason for offering diversity programmes; almost half said it was a business need, and another 38 percent saw it as a competitive issue. Hiring and promotion quotas may be corporate anathema, but at firms as diverse as Hughes Aircraft, Xerox, Colgate-Palmolive, and Levi Strauss diversity goals are a required part of annual performance reviews: with their own salaries and bonuses linked to those goals, managers have to take them seriously.

A tougher question is whether any of this makes a difference to corporate performance. Social-science research suggests that diversity can boost creativity, according to Taylor Cox of the University of Michigan Business School. In controlled experiments, homogeneous and ethnically diverse groups were assigned the same problem; the diverse groups did better because, he speculates, they drew from a broader spectrum of experience. There also appears to be a correlation between a company's innovativeness and its diversity.

The evidence is pretty thin, however. And there is little sign of a link between diversity programmes and profits. Yet the broader point is that, given America's fast-changing demographics, big firms cannot avoid having a diverse workforce even if they want to. And, since social tensions do not disappear when staff clock in for work, it makes sense to foster harmony in the workplace. In this context, what matters is not whether but how firms rethink their personnel policies—from recruitment, to flexible work practices, to medical coverage that reflects differing family structures.

The danger remains that these good intentions can turn into the rankest kind of race- and sex-counting, entrenching rather than dispelling prejudice. White men at a federal agency were understandably outraged last year [1994] when they were reportedly told to walk through a gauntlet of women who ranked their masculinity on a scale of one-to-ten. And a suspicion that favored groups are leapfrogging up the corporate ladder is a sure way to undermine morale. For diversity to be turned into a genuine competitive advantage, the bottom line must be that the right people are put in the right jobs. The early signs from corporate America are reasonably encouraging.

FIGHTING OVER THE SPOILS[5]

In 1983 a contractor named J. A. Croson submitted the lowest bid to outfit Richmond, Virginia's city jail with new urinals. To meet the city's quotas Croson was told to subcontract 30 percent of the job to firms owned by members of so-called ethnic minorities. Unable to meet this demand without losing money, Croson sued on the grounds that setting aside a percentage of government contracts for minorities violated his 14th Amendment right to equal protection.

In standing up for his rights, Croson inadvertently started a whole new industry—disparity studies. Whatever else the suit may accomplish, it has created lucrative work for a lot of self-anointed experts.

City of Richmond v. J. A. Croson reached the U.S. Supreme Court, and in 1989 the Court ruled that set-asides for officially favored groups were unconstitutional unless the municipality could prove that there was "significant statistical disparity between the number of qualified minority contractors willing and able" to do the work and the number of minority firms that received contracts. In other words, minority firms were not automatically entitled to the business. The city also had to show that the disparity was caused by discrimination.

[5]Article by Nina Munk, staff writer, from *Forbes* 154:50–1 Ag 15 '94. Reprinted by permission of FORBES Magazine © Forbes Inc., 1994.

But how to define "disparity"? You need an expert, of course. Already some sixty-five disparity studies have been produced, at prices that sometimes top $1 million per study. At least a dozen more are under way. The Supreme Court had also implicitly ruled that cites must keep their disparity studies up to date; old figures won't do. The city of Dallas is now spending $185,000 to update its 1992 disparity study. George LaNoue, director of the University of Maryland's policy sciences graduate program, estimates that, nationwide, taxpayers have spent $45 million on disparity studies.

Typical of the new profession is Atlanta-based D.J. Miller & Associates, which has completed thirteen disparity studies and is working on four more. Another leading disparity expert: National Economic Research Associates. The White Plains, NY-based firm has completed fifteen disparity studies and is now working on two, including a $1 million study for the state of Texas.

"It's a lucrative market," says D. J. Miller consultant Garry Blackwell. "It seems like every day we have new competition."

No surprise that most studies find what many local governments want them to show: that the place is rife with bias and discrimination. When Miami's disparity study, drawn up by KPMG Peat Marwick, found no clear discrimination against blacks or Hispanics, the city commission dumped Peat Marwick and sent its own staff off for more acceptable results. No report has been issued so far, and Miami has not changed its set-aside and quota policies.

"The goal of disparity studies is often to preserve the set-aside program," concludes University of Maryland's LaNoue, "not to identify and punish discrimination."

No surprise either that with more and more "disadvantaged" groups popping up all the time, the disparity studies have become a battleground among the various groups seeking handouts and special deals.

In Texas last year [1993] $371 million, or 8.3 percent of the state's $4.5 billion in contracts, went to what the politicians there call "historically underutilized businesses." Of that $371 million, 42 percent went to white women. That upset local blacks and Hispanics, who say white men simply use their wives as fronts to win set-aside bids.

. . . Hispanic activists in Dade County, FL, which encompasses Miami, demanded new quotas that would increase their numbers in the county's corrections department. Currently over 60 percent of the corrections department's employees are black. With budgets tight that can only mean blacks will have to step aside to make room for Hispanics.

Samuel Carradine, executive director of the 3,500-member National Association of Minority Contractors, says that as Asians and women have gained influence, the share of federally funded construction contracts awarded to blacks and Hispanics nationwide has dropped. He estimates that five years ago blacks and Hispanics got between 7 and 9 percent of the contracts; last year [1993], less than 3 percent.

Thus in New York State, for the fiscal year ended Mar. 31, [1994] 127 of 205 federally funded engineering subcontracts for minorities and women went to Asians. Another fifty-six went to women. Blacks got just fourteen contracts.

You can see what's happening in the U.S. Department of Transportation's federal highway contract program for what the DOT calls "disadvantaged businesses." In 1985 the DOT's highway pork awarded to minorities was worth about $1.6 billion; firms owned by blacks and American Indians got around half. Last year [1993] DOT's highway set-asides were worth $1.8 billion, but blacks and Indians got less than one-quarter.

Who did well? Hispanics increased their share of the DOT pie somewhat, from $334 million to $391 million, but firms owned by women did the best. Their share jumped from $307 million to $879 million.

Nowhere is the affirmative action tug-of-war more contentious than in California. According to recent Census Bureau estimates, 27 percent of the state's thirty-one million people are Hispanic (not counting illegal immigrants), 11.2 percent are Asian and 7.7 percent are black.

Not surprisingly, disparity studies are a big issue in California. A draft of Los Angeles' $400,000 disparity study that was leaked to the *Los Angeles Business Journal* in January[1994] suggested that blacks get more than their proportionate share of city contracts and may thus be ineligible for future set-aside contracts. That created angry outcries from those who presume to be speaking for blacks. So inflammatory is the subject that the report, originally due almost two years ago [1992], has yet to be released. Meanwhile, Hispanic activist and talk-radio host Xavier Hermosillo's routine mayoral appointment to the Los Angeles Fire Commission was rejected . . . after he asserted that blacks had too many Los Angeles City Hall jobs.

The fight for the loot sometimes turns bitter. Listen to Albert Lipscomb, a Dallas city councilman for nine years. "Historically," says Lipscomb, "we've had the Chicanos watch us from around the corner and, when we blacks have pried open the doors, then they've come in."

The National Association of Minority Contractors' Carradine has a solution: more pork. He blames the escalating bitterness in the affirmative action tug-of-war on too few set-aside programs, divided among too many "disadvantaged" groups. "By increasing the number of participants without increasing the size of the pie," says Carradine, "you're forcing these organizations to fight over crumbs."

To any honest observer the truth is clear: Affirmative action, at least in government, is just another form of patronage, dispensed with scant regard for merit.

Why is it surprising that people will quarrel about it—and seek to get into the act? Henry Mello, California Senate majority leader, recently introduced a bill to amend the state's definition of Hispanic to include Spaniards and Portuguese. In Texas, advocates for disabled people are demanding that people who use wheelchairs be considered legal minorities when bidding for state contracts. The Small Business Administration now includes Tongans, Indonesians, Sri Lankans, and Asian Indians in its list of socially disadvantaged groups. In Washington, Congress is considering making Arab-Americans an official minority.

When does comedy become tragedy?

A HAND UP, BUT NOT A HANDOUT[6]

When Gary L. Ennis went into the highway construction business in 1977, he figured that big-time road builders would pave a path to his door. As a Native American, Ennis could help Maine

[6]Article by Catherine Yang, staff writer, from March 27, 1995 issue of *BusinessWeek* 70-2. Copyright © 1995 by The McGraw-Hill Companies. Reprinted with permission. All rights reserved.

contractors meet their federally mandated goal of placing 10 percent of their highway business with minority- and women-owned companies. But he soon found himself in a rut: General contractors saw him as a quota-filler and relegated him to low-margin jobs. Or they helped women relatives and friends set up companies to get the work. "The big contractors found a way to meet the letter, but not the spirit, of the law," he says.

Disgusted, Ennis quit construction in 1988. But unlike the swelling ranks of affirmative-action foes, he thinks the programs should be reformed, not abandoned. "Racism is alive and well," says Ennis, now a parish administrator for Catholic Charities Maine in Caribou, ME. "It's a good idea to help people with a hand up, but not a handout."

His experience highlights the mixed record of affirmative action in federal contracting—America's quarter-century-old effort to help build a minority business class. A look at the minority contracting programs at the Small Business Administration and the Defense and Transportation Depts.[*] shows that these big "set-aside" and preference plans fall short of their goals.

As Ennis found, the programs are subject to abuse by white contractors using minority "front" companies. Federal agencies focus on meeting numerical goals and neglect the training that could help minority companies survive outside the sheltered world of government preferences. And the programs can create resentment by shutting out some struggling white-owned companies.

Prime Target. But where bureaucrats have provided technical support and advice as well as contracts, minority businesses have thrived. "You have to bring minority contractors into the business networks," says Timothy Bates, a Wayne State University professor and expert on minority contracting. "There has to be some effort to push back the barriers."

Such successes could get lost in the growing clamor to end affirmative action. GOP Presidential hopeful Senator Phil Gramm of Texas pledges to wipe out all federal "quotas, preferences, and set-asides." Senate majority leader Bob Dole, R-Kan., is scrutinizing the 166 federal preference programs identified by congressional researchers. President Clinton, scrambling to placate white voters without alienating blacks, has ordered his own review of affirmative action.

Public resentment often focuses on hiring preferences—the policy first mandated by President Johnson in a 1965 executive order that required government contractors to take "affirmative action" to hire and promote more women and minorities. But hiring policies are ultimately up to the private sector. The federal contracting programs, on the other hand, give agencies power to bend purchasing rules so that a small percentage of federal contracts goes to "disadvantaged" companies. It's those programs that are most vulnerable to the congressional ax.

The most criticized set-aside program is the Small Business Administration's 8(a) plan. Under the 1969 program, the SBA certifies 5,400 minority- and women-owned companies as "socially and economically disadvantaged." These companies—ranging from janitorial and construction to computer service outfits—can contract with federal agencies without competitive bidding.

The SBA is supposed to help these businesses develop survival skills during the nine years they can stay in the program. But 42 percent of the companies that graduated between 1990 and 1993 have folded or shrunk. Intended "to give minorities the license to hunt and to teach them to hunt," the plan is now "a hand-holding program," says Walter Larke Sorg, a Nixon administration official who helped found the 8(a) program. The SBA says the failure rate of 8(a) companies mirrors the rate for all small businesses. But in August [1994], it announced plans to beef up its mentoring efforts, a tacit admission that they were wanting.

Lucky Few. The lack of competitive bidding, even among themselves, keeps minority companies from learning the ropes. And federal agencies can play favorites rather than hassle with bidding. So a handful of companies ends up benefiting. In 1994, 1 percent of participating companies got 25 percent of the program's $4.4 billion pool, the General Accounting Office (GAO) found, while 56 percent got no contracts.

Some agencies will go to great lengths to stick with an 8(a) company they already know. A 1994 GAO study of an Energy Dept. office found that it shortened a contract's length and relaxed the requirement on skill levels to keep the price below the SBA's $3 million ceiling for noncompetitive awards to 8(a) companies. When that deal expired, the agency rehired the firm. Energy says it's now trying to use more companies.

In some agencies, minority programs have spurred bitter complaints from white, male-owned rivals that they're being squeezed out of the government market. The Defense Dept., for example, has set a seemingly modest goal of placing 5 percent of its vast contracts with disadvantaged businesses. But with 60 percent of the military's funds spent on aircraft, ships, and other big-ticket items, smaller contractors—white and minority—are crowded into such remaining areas as construction, computer services, and maintenance. Defense spends only 10.3 percent of its contracting budget on construction, for example, but gets 29.5 percent of its minority purchases in that sector.

Within those areas, Defense rules require purchasing officers to limit bidding to minority firms whenever such suppliers are available. The result can be painful for white contractors: Bob McCallie's engineering firm may lose the $150,000-plus computer management contract it has held since 1989 at the Air Force's Strategic Command near Omaha. The Air Force wants to switch the job, without bids, to a black-owned firm near St. Louis. Defense concedes its contracting causes problems: "Any program designed to favor one segment will, by definition, hurt others," says Tim J. Foreman, a procurement analyst.

When minority companies get the support they need, they can take off—without resentment from white-male companies. The Transportation Dept. asks the states to grant 10 percent of their federal highway money to minority- and women-owned businesses. Vermont sets a higher hurdle: Contractors there have to meet a 20 percent benchmark.

The state now boasts almost fifty successful minority- and women-owned companies that it helped cultivate. It spends only $5,000 a year on technical assistance—mostly on accounting courses—and gives informal advice to fledgling entrepreneurs. That apparently helps, judging from the number of companies that once got such advice and are now winning bids without special support. "A business should be competitive enough to get work without government incentives," says Lorena R. Laprade, president of L&D Safety Marketing Corp., a Berlin, VT, highway line-striping company that got breaks. The company has grown from three employees in 1985 to twenty-six. Proven track records like L&D's help alleviate resentment from companies that don't get assistance.

Worth the Gamble. Many of Vermont's general contractors hire minority- or women-owned companies, even after they have filled their quota, because "they have the expertise," says Kim Smalley of Pike Industries Inc., a highway-paving contractor in Tilton, NH. Vermont officials often promote such businesses across state lines. Augusta, Maine-based Bridgecorp hired African-American Jesse R. Watkin II to do the painting work on a $4.5 million Vermont bridge project even though it had met its minority requirement. Watkins was new to the painting business, but Vermont officials vouched for him. "We felt it was worth the gamble," says Ken Burrill, Bridgecorp's president.

The state of Vermont knows what American businesses have discovered, too: that buyers need to cultivate their suppliers to get the best performance. Similar attention from the federal government could help nurture the strong minority businesses it set out to seed thirty years ago. That would hasten the day when numerical goals and special preferences can fall by the wayside.

IV. THE NATIONAL DEBATE

Editor's Introduction

Although over the years politicians have threatened to curtail or dispense with affirmative action entirely, it is only now that the end of the program seems possible. Its abolition stands high on the right wing of the Republican party's agenda. Section Four of this volume brings together articles from both sides of the debate. In an essay in *Time*, Barbara Ehrenreich discusses the issue of discrimination against white males under affirmative action. While maintaining that competent white men should be hired over less competent women and minorities, Ehrenreich argues that racism, often in subliminal form, still persists in the workplace, and that the effect of affirmative action has on the whole been beneficial.

The attack on affirmative action by Ehrenreich is followed by two articles in defense of it by liberal writers—Adolph Reed, Jr. in *The Progressive* and Roger Wilkins in *The Nation*. Reed is critical of the idea of a strict meritocracy, since there is no objective measure that exists entirely apart from human prejudice and ideology. "The options," he concludes, "are not between affirmative action or some pristine world in which *merit* is its own reward, but between affirmative action or naked discrimination and exclusion." Wilkins also attacks "the myth that America is a meritocratic society," since money, family, and connections often count for much more than merit. White men, he claims, still control virtually everything while, according to the Urban Institute, 53 percent of black men aged 25-34 are either unemployed or earn too little to lift a family of four out of poverty.

The final piece treats affirmative action from a more philosophic perspective, and is notable for its keen observations. Nicolaus Lemann writing for *New York Times Magazine* has an historical orientation as he explores how affirmative action developed into a far-reaching program implementing quotas and sponsoring ever-increasing numbers of minorities, measures that were never part of its original mandate. Yet critical as Lemann is of affirmative action's faults, he supports it; because abolishing it without putting something else in its place would be to abandon our most vulnerable citizens.

PLANET OF THE WHITE GUYS[1]

On the planet inhabited by the anti-affirmative action activists, the only form of discrimination left is the kind that operates against white males. There, in the name of redressing ancient wrongs, white men are routinely shoved aside to make room for less qualified women and minorities. These favored ones have no problems at all—except for that niggling worry that their colleagues see them as under qualified "affirmative-action babies." Maybe there was once an evil called racism in this charmed place—thirty or three hundred years ago, that is—but it's been replaced by affirmative action.

Now I agree that discrimination is an ugly thing no matter who's at the receiving end, and that it may be worth reviewing affirmative action, as President Clinton has proposed, to see whether it's been fairly applied. People should not be made to suffer for the wicked things perpetrated by their ancestors or by those who merely looked like them. Competent white men should be hired over less competent women and minorities, otherwise, sooner or later, the trains won't run on time and the planes will fall down from the sky.

But it would be a shame if Clinton's "review" sidesteps the undeniable persistence of racism in the workplace and just about everywhere else. Consider the recent lesson from Rutgers University. Here we have a perfectly nice liberal fellow, a college president with a record of responsiveness to minority concerns. He opens his mouth to talk about minority test scores, and then—like a Tourette's syndrome victim in the grip of a seizure—he comes out with the words "genetic hereditary background." Translated from the academese: minorities are dumb, and they're dumb because they're born that way.

[1]Article by Barbara Ehrenreich, staff writer, from *Time* 145:114 Mr 13 '95.

Can we be honest here? I've been around white folks most of my life—from left-wingers to right-wingers, from crude-mouthed louts to prissy-minded elitists—and I've heard enough to know that *The Bell Curve* is just a long-winded version of what an awful lot of white people actually believe. Take a look, for example, at a survey reported by the National Opinion Research Center in 1991, which found a majority of whites asserting that minorities are lazier, more violence-prone and less intelligent than whites. Even among the politically correct, the standard praise word for a minority person is "articulate," as if to say, "Isn't it amazing how well he can speak!"

Prejudice of the quiet, subliminal kind doesn't flow from the same place as hate. All you have to do to be infected is look around: at the top of the power hierarchy—filling more than 90 percent of top corporate-leadership slots and a grossly disproportionate share of managerial and professional positions—you see white men. Meanwhile, you tend to find minorities clustered in the kind of menial roles—busing dishes, unloading trucks—that our parents warned were waiting for us too if we didn't get our homework done.

So what is the brain to make of this data? It does what brains are designed to do: it simplifies and serves up the quickie generalizations that are meant to guide us through a complex world. Thus when we see a black colleague, who may be an engineer or a judge, the brain, in its innocence, announces helpfully, "Janitor-type approaching, wearing a suit."

Maybe it's easier for a woman to acknowledge this because subliminal prejudice hurts women too. Studies have shown, for example, that people are more likely to find an article convincing if it is signed by "Bob Someone" instead of, say, "Barbara Someone." It's just the brain's little habit of parceling reality into tidy equations, such as female equals probable fluffhead. The truth is that each of us carries around an image of competence in our mind, and its face is neither female nor black. Hence our readiness to believe, whenever we hear of a white male losing out to a minority or a woman, that the white guy was actually more qualified. In Jesse Helms' winning 1990 campaign commercial, a white man crumples up a rejection letter, while the voice-over reminds him that he was "the best-qualified." But was he? Is he always? And why don't we ever hear a white guy worry out loud that his colleagues suspect he got the job—as white men have for centuries—in part because he's male and white?

It's a measure of the ambient racism that we find it so hard to believe that affirmative action may actually be doing something right: ensuring that the best guy gets the job, regardless of that guy's race or sex. Eventually, when the occupational hierarchy is so thoroughly integrated that it no longer makes sense for our subconscious minds to invest the notion of competence with a particular skin color or type of genitalia, affirmative action can indeed be cast aside like training wheels.

Meanwhile, aggrieved white men can console themselves with the gains their wives have made. Numerically speaking, white women are the biggest beneficiaries of affirmative action, and because white women tend to marry white men, it follows that white men are, numerically speaking, among the top beneficiaries too. On this planet, Bob Dole and Pat Buchanan may not have been able to figure that out yet, but most white guys, I like to think, are plenty smart enough.

ASSAULT ON AFFIRMATIVE ACTION[2]

Not long ago I rode on the train back from Detroit within earshot of a white, freelance electrician who works for an international corporate temp agency. In the course of chatting about his work with another white passenger, he complained that his Detroit job had been hampered by the rest of his crew. He knew from the time they showed up that they would be a problem, he said, because, "First of all, one of them was Puerto Rican." Nearly everyone else on the car was black, so he may have felt constrained to let the Puerto Rican stand in for other minorities. He then talked disparagingly about how the crew members comported themselves raucously in hotel restaurants and bars—saying nothing at all about the quality of their work.

Later in the conversation, the electrician recounted an incident from a different job, in which a co-worker and buddy locked a donkey in a hotel room as a practical joke. The result was considerable property damage, but he narrated the tale with good humor, as boys-will-be-boys hijinks.

[2]Article by Adolph Reed, Jr., co-chair of the Coalition for New Priorities, from *The Progressive* 59:18–20 Je 3 '95. Copyright © 1995. Reprinted with permission.

This anecdote underscores a problem that permeates American society and has consequences for many public debates—ranging from affirmative action to capital punishment to welfare: the same or comparable actions are judged differently, depending on the racial identities of the action.

Now that the Republicans and their right-wing Democratic allies have chosen to make affirmative action their racist "wedge issue" of the year, constructing a reasonable, honest, and progressive perspective on affirmative action is particularly important.

Fundamental to the argument against affirmative action is the view that it makes tradeoffs between merit and quotas.

This view rests on two key premises: 1) that it is possible to isolate in the practical world of human choices some pure or absolute notion of merit; and 2) that the criteria that determined access to jobs and schools before the advent of affirmative action depended on such a notion of pure merit.

Of course, there is no idea of merit that is innocent of prejudice. Despite all the blather about "reverse discrimination," the closer we get to real cases, the clearer it is that work, school, and our public spaces are still full of precisely the sorts of exclusionist behavior that civil-rights enforcement seeks to overcome.

Employers and supervisors base their decisions on considerations that include the extent to which they feel comfortable with a given candidate, their sense of how an individual would "fit" in the workplace situation, and on vague feelings and prior assumptions about candidates' general abilities.

As with the electrician, those assumptions are likely to be influenced by racial or gender stereotypes. Not surprisingly, several studies using discrimination "testers" (pairs of applicants matched on all obviously pertinent characteristics except race) recently have demonstrated that, when black and white candidates are identically qualified on paper, blacks are likely to be rejected in favor of whites for jobs, housing, even automobile purchases.

There is no objective measure that exists entirely apart from human prejudice and ideology.

Early psychometricians interpreted the finding that women performed better than men on some components of IQ tests as evidence of flawed design and adjusted the tests accordingly. Why? Because they presumed from the outset that men are smarter than women and that, therefore, a test result that showed the opposite had to have been structured poorly.

Similarly, Stephen Jay Gould's *Mismeasure of Man* documents the history of "race" researchers' revisions, often inversions, of their indicators of biological superiority upon finding that blacks seemed to score higher than whites on some tests. Pure, "scientific" reasoning decreed that the measures—say, relative lack of body hair—couldn't really indicate preeminence because blacks were clearly inferior.

Women are no longer (at least for the moment) presumed automatically to be less intelligent than men. In fact, intelligence testers have for some time crafted tests to correct for gross gender differences in results. But race differences don't set off the same alarms, because the idea of racial equality in intelligence hasn't yet attained the status of an automatic, incontrovertible assumption. This distinction is highlighted by the fact that the eugenicist book *The Bell Curve* within four months of publication sold 400,000 copies, and has been treated as respectable science by all-too-many pundits and academics.

The lesson here with respect to affirmative action is that even ostensibly neutral measures can be freighted with prejudice. That is why the U.S. Supreme Court in the 1971 *Griggs v. Duke Power* decision ruled that employers can use hiring and promotion standards that disproportionately exclude blacks only if they can demonstrate that those standards specifically measure the ability to get the job done. (*Bell Curve* authors Charles Murray and Richard Herrnstein attacked the *Griggs* decision early and often.)

It is unquestionably true that until the 1960s blacks directly and explicitly on racial grounds were denied access to public contracts and commercial credit. The effect was that whites enjoyed a competitive advantage that facilitated success in general and gave them a racial monopoly on public contracting in particular.

The same holds for many categories of employment. A white police officer, hired before affirmative action, as likely as not owed his employment and subsequent promotions in part to the existence of a racial and gender monopoly that limited the field against which he had to compete. A white carpenter who belonged to a union that didn't allow black or female members was in the same position.

The benefits accruing from this preferential access to desirable employment, moreover, extend through other aspects of life—from ability to accumulate capital in the form of home ownership and education to, beginning with the New Deal, eligibility for those forms of social welfare targeted to stably employed whites. Employment discrimination intensifies housing inequality, which reinforces unequal access to the political system and public policy, which reinforces unequal access to social resources, which intensifies income inequality, and so on and on.

That beneficiaries of these preferences may have worked hard for their attainments does not negate the equally significant fact that their efforts have been aided by the direct, indirect, and cumulative effects of the exclusion of others no less worthy than they.

Still, affirmative-action foes argue that specific efforts to correct for racial bias fly in the face of "fairness." The relative absence of minorities and women from attractive jobs, and the fact that they are clustered in unattractive positions should not, they say, be taken as evidence of discrimination. The logic of this view is that equal opportunity is guaranteed simply by proclaiming a policy of non-discrimination. Anything beyond that—like setting specific goals and standards to overcome discrimination— amounts to mandating quota systems, they say. And quotas reject "merit."

This complaint has a long, nefarious history. Supreme Court Justice Joseph Bradley's opinion in the 1883 decision overturning the 1875 Civil Rights Act proclaimed—eighteen years after the end of slavery and in the midst of the terrorist reimposition of white supremacy in the South—that it was time that the black American "takes the rank of a mere citizen, and ceases to be the special favorite of the laws."

At bottom, this perspective assumes that the real-world dynamics that concentrate advantages among whites or men don't mean a thing about equal opportunity. Systemic white or male privilege is presumed to be a reasonable, natural expression of merit. This at least verges on an assumption of inherent white, male superiority.

The acceptance of white, male social privilege as natural lay behind Reagan and Bush administrations' lawsuits challenging affirmative-action plaintiffs to show an actual intent to discriminate—a requirement that is practically impossible to satisfy.

The Supreme Court majority in recent years has relied on an intent standard and has disregarded history and social context in a number of civil-rights rulings. The *City of Mobile v. Bolden* ruling in 1980 upheld the city's use of an at-large electoral system, even though no blacks had been able to win seats on the city council. The Court held that black underrepresentation could not be taken as sufficient evidence of discrimination. Alabama's—and Mobile's own—segregationist history, according to this interpretation, is irrelevant. The burden lay with those claiming exclusion to prove discriminatory intent.

The 1989 *Richmond v. J. A. Croson* ruling extended this logic to affirmative action in municipal contracting. In throwing out the city's minority set-aside program, the Court ruled that a pattern of extreme underrepresentation (blacks made up more than 50 percent of the population, and fewer than 1 percent of contractors) doesn't constitute evidence of entrenched patterns of exclusion sufficient to justify extraordinary measures to create equality of opportunity.

The 1992 *Shaw v. Reno* ruling made a comparable argument in throwing out the Congressional-reapportionment scheme that made it possible to elect the first black representatives in this century from North Carolina—a state that as recently as the late 1960s was home to more Ku Klux Klansmen than any other. And in its current session, the Court—in ruling for white firefighters claiming reverse discrimination as a result of a municipal hiring and promotion plan aimed at approaching parity in black representation—treated as irrelevant even the particularly sordid white-supremacist history of Birmingham, AL.

To defend these illogical decisions, opponents of affirmative action have seized on a set of misleading arguments that revolve around the theme that affirmative action actually is self-defeating. One such claim is that affirmative action stigmatizes its beneficiaries as unqualified and therefore *creates* racist stereotypes, resentment, and thus discrimination. Another is that it instills in those beneficiaries debilitating doubts about both their competence and their white, male colleagues' perceptions of their abilities. Yet another is that affirmative action actually restricts opportunity for minorities and women by slotting them into narrow quotas.

The notion that affirmative action creates racism is an old chestnut; it has been applied to every initiative undertaken in support of racial equality from the 14th Amendment to the *Brown* decision and the 1964 Civil Rights Act. It collapses before the simple fact that widespread racist practices prompted anti-discrimination efforts in the first place.

The claim that affirmative action is intended to compensate for past suffering—a kind of reparations—has become conventional and is even bandied about by ostensibly progressive pundits. This formulation gives rise to diatribes about how much whose immigrant grandparents suffered themselves and how many of them owned slaves and other such pointless blather.

But the purpose of affirmative action is to remove fetters on equality of opportunity by attacking *existing* patterns of inequality that originate from current discrimination and the cumulative results of past exclusion and discrimination.

Opponents now often claim that affirmative action is ineffective because it mainly benefits the well-off. But studies by Martin Carnoy (in his 1994 book, *Faded Dreams*) and Jonathan Leonard (in the *Review of Economics and Statistics and the Journal of Human Resources*) find a significant positive effect of anti-discrimination efforts for *all* skill levels among black Americans. And anecdotal information certainly supports those findings.

In the academic world, anti-discrimination policies have induced admissions committees to look more closely at pools of students who would earlier have been dismissed out of hand. And affirmative-action guidelines for faculty-hiring practices have been largely responsible for proliferation of open, nationally advertised searches and regularized procedures that break down nepotism and inbreeding.

The most visible recent "reverse discrimination" controversy illustrates the weakness of the anti-affirmative-action position in academia. In a case currently pending, *Cheryl J. Hopwood v. University of Texas Law School*, it turns out that race was not a salient factor. The alleged victims were unlikely to have been admitted even if no blacks or Latinos had applied. Their academic records in fact were mediocre. The plain fact is that the charge of special preferences is a smokescreen.

The options are not affirmative action or some pristine world in which "merit" is its own reward, but affirmative action or naked discrimination and exclusion.

RACISM HAS ITS PRIVILEGES[3]

The storm that has been gathering over affirmative action for the past few years has burst. Two conservative California professors are leading a drive to place an initiative on the state ballot in 1996 that will ask Californians to vote affirmative action up or down. Since the state is beloved in political circles for its electoral votes, advance talk of the initiative has put the issue high on the national agenda. Three Republican presidential contenders— Bob Dole, Phil Gramm and Lamar Alexander—have already begun taking shots at various equal opportunity programs. Congressional review of the Clinton administration's enforcement of these programs has begun. The President has started his own review, promising adherence to principles of nondiscrimination and full opportunity while asserting the need to prune those programs that are unfair or malfunctioning.

It is almost an article of political faith that one of the major influences in last November's 1994 election was the backlash against affirmative action among "angry white men," who are convinced it has stacked the deck against them. Their attitudes are shaped and their anger heightened by unquestioned and virtually uncheckable anecdotes about victimized whites flooding the culture. For example, *Washington Post* columnist Richard Cohen recently began what purported to be a serious analysis and attack on affirmative action by recounting that he had once missed out on a job someplace because they "needed a woman."

Well, I have an anecdote too, and it, together with Cohen's, offers some important insights about the debate that has flared recently around the issues of race, gender, and justice. Some years ago, after watching me teach as a visiting professor for two semesters, members of the history department at George Mason University invited me to compete for a full professorship and endowed chair. Mason, like other institutions in Virginia's higher education system, was under a court order to desegregate. I went through the appropriate application and review process and, in due course, was appointed. A few years later, not long after I had

[3]Article by Roger Wilkins, a professor of history at George Madison University, from *The Nation* 260:409-10 Mr 27, '95. Copyright © 1995 by The Nation Company, L.P. Reprinted with permission.

been honored as one of the university's distinguished professors, I was shown an article by a white historian asserting that he had been a candidate for that chair but that at the last moment the job had been whisked away and handed to an unqualified black. I checked the story and discovered that this fellow had, in fact, applied but had not even passed the first threshold. But his "reverse discrimination" story is out there polluting the atmosphere in which this debate is taking place.

Affirmative action, as I understand it, was not designed to punish anyone; it was, rather—as a result of a clear-eyed look at how America actually works—an attempt to enlarge opportunity for *everybody*. As amply documented in the 1968 Kerner Commission report on racial disorders, when left to their own devices, American institutions in such areas as college admissions, hiring decisions and loan approvals had been making choices that discriminated against blacks. That discrimination, which flowed from doing what came naturally, hurt more than blacks: It hurt the entire nation, as the riots of the late 1960s demonstrated. Though the Kerner report focused on blacks, similar findings could have been made about other minorities and women.

Affirmative action required institutions to develop plans enabling them to go beyond business as usual and search for qualified people in places where they did not ordinarily conduct their searches or their business. Affirmative action programs generally require some proof that there has been a good-faith effort to follow the plan and numerical guidelines against which to judge the sincerity and the success of the effort. The idea of affirmative action is *not* to force people into positions for which they are unqualified but to encourage institutions to develop realistic criteria for the enterprise at hand and then to find a reasonably diverse mix of people qualified to be engaged in it. Without the requirements calling for plans, good-faith efforts and the setting of broad numerical goals, many institutions would do what they had always done: assert that they had looked but "couldn't find anyone qualified," and then go out and hire the white man they wanted to hire in the first place.

Affirmative action has done wonderful things for the United States by enlarging opportunity and developing and utilizing a far broader array of the skills available in the American population than in the past. It has not outlived its usefulness. It was never designed to be a program to eliminate poverty. It has not always been used wisely, and some of its permutations do have to be reconsidered, refined or, in some cases, abandoned. It is not a quota program, and those cases where rigid numbers are used (except under a court or administrative order after a specific finding of discrimination) are a bastardization of an otherwise highly beneficial set of public policies.

President Clinton is right to review what is being done under present laws and to express a willingness to eliminate activities that either don't work or are unfair. Any program that has been in place for thirty years should be reviewed. Getting rid of what doesn't work is both good government and good politics. Gross abuses of affirmative action provide ammunition for its opponents and undercut the moral authority of the entire effort. But the President should retain—and strengthen where required—those programs necessary to enlarge social justice.

What makes the affirmative action issue so difficult is that it engages blacks and whites exactly at those points where they differ the most. There are some areas, such as rooting for the local football team, where their experiences and views are virtually identical. There are others—sometimes including work and school—where their experiences and views both overlap and diverge. And finally, there are areas such as affirmative action and inextricably related notions about the presence of racism in society where the divergences draw out almost all the points of difference between the races.

This Land Is My Land

Blacks and whites experience America very differently. Though we often inhabit the same space, we operate in very disparate psychic spheres.

Whites have an easy sense of ownership of the country; they feel they are entitled to receive all that is best in it. Many of them believe that their country—though it may have some faults—is superior to all others and that, as Americans, they are superior as well. Many of them think of this as a white country and some of them even experience it that way. They think of it as a land of opportunity—a good place with a lot of good people in it. Some suspect (others *know*) that the presence of blacks messes everything up.

To blacks there's nothing very easy about life in America, and any sense of ownership comes hard because we encounter so much resistance in making our way through the ordinary occurrences of life. And I'm not even talking here about overt acts of discrimination but simply about the way whites intrude on and disturb our psychic space without even thinking about it.

A telling example of this was given to me by a black college student in Oklahoma. He said whites give him looks that say: "What are, you doing here?"

"When do they give you that look?" I asked.

"Every time I walk in a door," he replied.

When he said that, every black person in the room nodded and smiled in a way that indicated recognition based on thousands of such moments in their own lives.

For most blacks, America is either a land of denied opportunity or one in which the opportunities are still grudgingly extended and extremely limited. For some—that one-third who are mired in poverty, many of them isolated in dangerous ghettos—America is a land of desperadoes and desperation. In places where whites see a lot of idealism, blacks see, at best, idealism mixed heavily with hypocrisy. Blacks accept America's greatness, but are unable to ignore ugly warts that many whites seem to need not to see. I am reminded here of James Baldwin's searing observation from *The Fire Next Time*:

The American Negro has the great advantage of having never believed that collection of myths to which white Americans cling: that their ancestors were all freedom-loving heroes, that they were born in the greatest country the world has ever seen, or that Americans are invincible in battle and wise in peace, that Americans have always dealt honorably with Mexicans and Indians and all other neighbors or inferiors, that American men are the world's most direct and virile, that American women are pure.

It goes without saying, then, that blacks and whites remember America differently. The past is hugely important since we argue a lot about who we are on the basis of who we think we have been, and we derive much of our sense of the future from how we think we've done in the past. In a nation in which few people know much history these are perilous arguments, because in such a vacuum, people tend to weave historical fables tailored to their political or psychic needs.

Blacks are still recovering the story of their role in America, which so many white historians simply ignored or told in ways that made black people ashamed. But in a culture that batters us, learning the real history is vital in helping blacks feel fully human. It also helps us understand just how deeply American we are, how richly we have given, how much has been taken from us and how much has yet to be restored. Supporters of affirmative action believe that broad and deep damage has been done to American culture by racism and sexism over the whole course of American history and that they are still powerful forces today. We believe that minorities and women are still disadvantaged in our highly competitive society and that affirmative action is absolutely necessary to level the playing field.

Not all white Americans oppose this view and not all black Americans support it. There are a substantial number of whites in this country who have been able to escape our racist and sexist past and to enter fully into the quest for equal justice. There are other white Americans who are not racists but who more or less passively accept the powerful suggestions coming at them from all points in the culture that whites are entitled to privilege and to freedom from competition with blacks. And then there are racists who just don't like blacks or who actively despise us. There are still others who may or may not feel deep antipathy, but who know how to manipulate racism and white anxiety for their own ends. Virtually all the people in the last category oppose affirmative action and some of them make a practice of preying upon those in the second category who are not paying attention or who, like the *Post's* Richard Cohen, are simply confused.

The Politics of Denial

One of these political predators is Senate majority leader Bob Dole. In his offhandedly lethal way, Dole delivered a benediction of "let me now forgive us" on *Meet the Press* recently. After crediting affirmative action for the 62 percent of the white male vote garnered by the Republicans, he remarked that slavery was "before we were born" and wondered whether future generations ought to have to continue "paying a price" for those ancient wrongs.

Such a view holds that whatever racial problems we once may have had have been solved over the course of the past thirty years and that most of our current racial friction is caused by racial and gender preferences that almost invariably work to displace some "qualified" white male. Words and phrases like "punish" or "preference" or "reverse discrimination" or "quota" are dropped into the discourse to buttress this view, as are those anecdotes about injustice to whites. Proponents of affirmative action see these arguments as disingenuous but ingenious because they reduce serious and complex social, political, economic, historical, and psychological issues to bumpersticker slogans designed to elicit Pavlovian responses.

The fact is that the successful public relations assault on affirmative action flows on a river of racism that is as broad, powerful, and American as the Mississippi. And, like the Mississippi, racism can be violent and deadly and is a permanent feature of American life. But while nobody who is sane denies the reality of the Mississippi, millions of Americans who are deemed sane—some of whom are powerful and some even thought wise—deny, wholly or in part, that racism exists.

It is critical to understand the workings of denial in this debate because it is used to obliterate the facts that created the need for the remedy in the first place. One of the best examples of denial was provided recently by the nation's most famous former history professor, House Speaker Newt Gingrich. According to the *Washington Post*, "Gingrich dismissed the argument that the beneficiaries of affirmative action, commonly African Americans, have been subjected to discrimination over a period of centuries. 'That is true of virtually every American,' Gingrich said, noting that the Irish were discriminated against by the English, for example."

That is breathtaking stuff coming from somebody who should know that blacks have been on this North American continent for 375 years and that for 245 the country permitted slavery. Gingrich should also know that for the next hundred years we had legalized subordination of blacks, under a suffocating blanket of condescension and frequently enforced by nightriding terrorists. We've had only thirty years of something else.

That something else is a nation trying to lift its ideals out of a thick, often impenetrable slough of racism. Racism is a hard word for what over the centuries became second nature in America—preferences across the board for white men and, following in their wake, white women. Many of these men seem to feel that it is un-American to ask them to share anything with blacks—particularly their work, their neighborhoods or "their" women.

To protect these things—apparently essential to their identity—
they engage in all forms of denial. For a historian to assert that
"virtually every American" shares the history I have just outlined
comes very close to lying.

Denial of racism is much like the denials that accompany ad-
dictions to alcohol, drugs, or gambling. It is probably not stretch-
ing the analogy too much to suggest that many racist whites are
so addicted to their unwarranted privileges and so threatened by
the prospect of losing them that all kinds of defenses become acceptable, including insistent distortions of reality in the form of
hypocrisy, lying or the most outrageous political demagogy.

Those People Don't Deserve Help

The demagogues have reverted to a new version of quite an
old trick. Before the 1950s, whites who were busy denying that
the nation was unfair to blacks would simply assert that we didn't
deserve equal treatment because we were *inferior*. These days it
is not permissible in most public circles to say that blacks are inferior, but it is perfectly acceptable to target the *behavior* of blacks,
specifically poor blacks. The argument then follows a fairly pre-
dictable line: The behavior of poor blacks requires a severe rethinking of national social policy, it is said. Advantaged blacks
really don't need affirmative action anymore, and when they are
the objects of such programs, some qualified white person (unqualified white people don't show up in these arguments) is (as
Dole might put it) "punished." While it is possible that color-blind
affirmative action programs benefiting all disadvantaged Americans are needed, those (i.e., blacks) whose behavior is so distress-
ing must be punished by restricting welfare, shriveling the safety
net, and expanding the prison opportunity. All of that would presumably give us, in William Bennett's words, "what we want—a
color-blind society," for which the white American psyche is presumably fully prepared.

There are at least three layers of unreality in these precepts.
The first is that the United States is not now and probably never
will be a color-blind society. It is the most color-conscious society
on earth. Over the course of 375 years, whites have given blacks
absolutely no reason to believe that they can behave in a color-
blind manner. In many areas of our lives—particularly in employment, housing and education—affirmative action is required to
counter deeply ingrained racist patterns of behavior.

Second, while I don't hold the view that all blacks who behave badly are blameless victims of a brutal system, I do believe that many poor blacks have, indeed, been brutalized by our culture, and I know of *no* blacks, rich or poor, who haven't been hurt in some measure by the racism in this country. The current mood (and, in some cases like the Speaker's, the cultivated ignorance) completely ignores the fact that some blacks never escaped the straight line of oppression that ran from slavery through the semi-slavery of sharecropping to the late mid-century migration from Southern farms into isolated pockets of urban poverty. Their families have always been excluded, poor, and without skills, and so they were utterly defenseless when the enormous American economic dislocations that began in the mid-1970s slammed into their communities, followed closely by deadly waves of crack cocaine. One would think that the double-digit unemployment suffered consistently over the past two decades by blacks who were *looking for work* would be a permanent feature of the discussions about race, responsibility, welfare, and rights.

But a discussion of the huge numbers of black workers who are becoming economically redundant would raise difficult questions about the efficiency of the economy at a time when millions of white men feel insecure. Any honest appraisal of unemployment would reveal that millions of low-skilled white men were being severely damaged by corporate and Federal Reserve decisions; it might also refocus the anger of those whites in the middle ranks whose careers have been shattered by the corporate downsizing fad.

But people's attention is kept trained on the behavior of some poor blacks by politicians and television news shows, reinforcing the stereotypes of blacks as dangerous, as threats, as unqualified. Frightened whites direct their rage at pushy blacks rather than at the corporations that export manufacturing operations to low-wage countries, or at the Federal Reserve, which imposes interest rate hikes that slow down the economy.

Who Benefits? We All Do

There is one final denial that blankets all the rest. It is that only society's "victims"—blacks, other minorities and women (who should, for God's sake, renounce their victimological outlooks)—have been injured by white male supremacy. Viewed in this light, affirmative action remedies are a kind of zero-sum game in which only the "victims" benefit. But racist and sexist whites who are not able to accept the full humanity of other people are themselves badly damaged—morally stunted—people. The principal product of a racist and sexist society is damaged people and institutions—victims and victimizers alike. Journalism and education, two enterprises with which I am familiar, provide two good examples.

Journalistic institutions often view the nation through a lens that bends reality to support white privilege. A recent issue of *U.S. News & World Report* introduced a package of articles on these issues with a question on its cover: "Does affirmative action mean No White Men Need Apply?" The words "No white men need apply" were printed in red against a white background and were at least four times larger than the other words in the question. Inside, the lead story was illustrated by a painting that carries out the cover theme, with a wan white man separated from the opportunity ladders eagerly being scaled by women and dark men. And the story yielded up the following sentence: "Affirmative action poses a conflict between two cherished American principles: the belief that all Americans deserve equal opportunities and the idea that hard work and merit, not race or religion or gender or birthright, should determine who prospers and who does not."

Whoever wrote that sentence was in the thrall of one of the myths that Baldwin was talking about. The sentence suggests—as many people do when talking about affirmative action—that America is a meritocratic society. But what kind of meritocracy excludes women and blacks and other minorities from all meaningful competition? And even in the competition among white men, money, family, and connections often count for much more than merit, test results (for whatever they're worth) and hard work.

The *U.S. News* story perpetuates and strengthens the view that many of my white students absorb from their parents: that white men now have few chances in this society. The fact is that white men still control virtually everything in America except the wealth held by widows. According to the Urban Institute, 53 percent of black men aged 25–34 are either unemployed or earn too little to lift a family of four from poverty.

Educational institutions that don't teach accurately about why America looks the way it does and why the distribution of winners and losers is as it is also injure our society. Here is another anecdote.

A warm, brilliant young white male student of mine came in just before he was to graduate and said that my course in race, law, and culture, which he had just finished, had been the most valuable and the most disturbing he had ever taken. I asked how it had been disturbing.

"I learned that my two heroes are racists," he said.

"Who are your heroes and how are they racists?" I asked.

"My mom and dad," he said. "After thinking about what I was learning, I understood that they had spent all my life making me into the same kind of racists they were."

Affirmative action had brought me together with him when he was 22. Affirmative action puts people together in ways that make that kind of revelation possible. Nobody is a loser when that happens. The country gains.

And that, in the end, is the case for affirmative action. The arguments supporting it should be made on the basis of its broad contributions to the entire American community. It is insufficient to vilify white males and to skewer them as the whiners that journalism of the kind practiced by *U.S. News* invites us to do. These are people who, from the beginning of the Republic, have been taught that skin color is destiny and that whiteness is to be revered. Listen to Jefferson, writing in the year the Constitution was drafted:

The first difference that strikes us is that of colour. . . . And is the difference of no importance? Is it not the foundation of a greater or less share of beauty in the two races? Are not the mixtures of red and white . . . in the one, preferable to that eternal monotony, which reigns in the countenances, that immoveable veil of black which covers all the emotions of the other race? Add to these, flowing hair, a more elegant symmetry of form, their own judgment in favor of the whites, declared by their preference for them, as uniformly as is the preference of the Oran-ootan for the black women over those of his own species. The circumstance of superior beauty, is thought worthy attention in the propagation of our horses, dogs, and other domestic animals; why not in that of man?

In a society so conceived and so dedicated, it is understandable that white males would take their preferences as a matter of natural right and consider any alteration of that a primal offense.

But a nation that operates in that way abandons its soul and its economic strength, and will remain mired in ugliness and moral squalor because so many people are excluded from the possibility of decent lives and from forming any sense of community with the rest of society.

Seen only as a corrective for ancient wrongs, affirmative action may be dismissed by the likes of Gingrich, Gramm, and Dole, just as attempts to federalize decent treatment of the freed slaves were dismissed after Reconstruction more than a century ago. Then, striking down the Civil Rights Act of 1875, Justice Joseph Bradley wrote of blacks that "there must be some stage in the progress of his elevation when he takes the rank of a mere citizen, and ceases to be the special favorite of the laws, and when his rights, as a citizen or a man, are to be protected in the ordinary modes by which other men's rights are protected."

But white skin has made some citizens—particularly white males—*the special favorites of the culture*. It may be that we will need affirmative action until most white males are really ready for a color-blind society—that is, when they are ready to assume "the rank of a mere citizen." As a nation we took a hard look at that special favoritism thirty years ago. Though the centuries of cultural preference enjoyed by white males still overwhelmingly skew power and wealth their way, we have in fact achieved a more meritocratic society as a result of affirmative action than we have ever previously enjoyed in this country.

If we want to continue making things better in this society, we'd better figure out ways to protect and defend affirmative action against the confused, the frightened, the manipulators and, yes, the liars in politics, journalism, education, and wherever else they may be found. In the name of longstanding American prejudice and myths and in the service of their own narrow interests, power-lusts, or blindness, they are truly victimizing the rest of us, perverting the ideals they claim to stand for and destroying the nation they pretend to serve.

TAKING AFFIRMATIVE ACTION APART[4]

Compton is a mostly black and Hispanic, down-at-the-heels, inner-ring suburb of Los Angeles known to the outside world mainly as the home of rap groups like N.W.A. (Niggas With Attitude—its first album was "Straight Outta Compton"). On a quiet blue-collar street of tract houses with lawns that need mowing stands, incongruously, a fancy new house with a BMW parked in its bricked front courtyard. There's a touch of Graceland about it, the poor boy's mansion. Inside the front door is a large, round marble-floored entrance foyer overlooked by a balcony. There is a swimming pool in the backyard.

The house belongs to Dr. Patrick Chavis, a forty-three-year-old obstetrician-gynecologist with an enormous practice comprising entirely poor people on Medicaid. Chavis is where he is because he was swept up in a historical tide. He is a beneficiary of affirmative action. In 1973, he and four other African Americans were admitted, under a special minorities-only program, to the University of California Medical School at Davis. Although all of the five were good students, medical-school admission is extremely competitive and none would have been admitted purely on the basis of undergraduate records. They got in because they were black, and therefore took the places of five white applicants with better grades and test scores.

One of these was a young engineer named Allan Bakke. He sued the medical school for discriminating against him on the basis of his race. The case went to the Supreme Court, resulting in its best-known decision to date on affirmative action: In June 1978, Bakke was ordered admitted (he too is a doctor today) and the special program was abolished. The Court also ruled, however, that universities could make being a minority a plus factor in their admissions decisions. *Bakke v. Regents of the University of California* was, then, an endorsement of affirmative action, but an extremely limited one. In the years following the decision, U.C.-Davis medical school admitted fewer blacks. Post-*Bakke*, Patrick Chavis couldn't have become a poor-folks' doctor.

[4]Article by Nicholas Lemann, author, from *The New York Times Magazine* 36–43 Je 11 '95. Copyright © 1995 by Nicholas Lemann. Reprinted with permission.

Four hundred miles north of Compton lies Berkeley, a beautiful small city that is home to what is probably the finest institution of public education in the United States, the University of California at Berkeley. In a drowsy neighborhood of graduate-student housing and organic grocery stores there is a shabby-genteel bungalow owned by one of those left-liberal cause organizations that spring up in university towns, the World Without War Council. The address is 1730 Martin Luther King Jr. Way. Improbably, the California chapter of the National Association of Scholars, an anti-P.C. organization, has its office upstairs in a tiny sublet space.

This year, the bungalow has been the site of occasional media stakeouts because it is the unofficial headquarters of a citizen initiative that would abolish in California precisely what the *Bakke* decision let stand—giving some measure of preference to black (and other minority) applicants in the name of promoting diversity. The fathers of the initiative, Tom Wood and Glynn Custred, are middle-aged white academics. Wood, a philosopher by training, has spent most of his career moving from short-term job to short-term job; he is now executive director of the California Association of Scholars. Custred is a tenured professor of anthropology at California State University at Hayward, down the road from Berkeley.

Custred is a friendly man with a fringe of white hair, a broad open face and searchlight blue eyes—a true believer. He was born in Birmingham, AL, during the Jim Crow era. His father was a steelworker who became a white-collar employee at the local gas company. When he was 14, the family moved to Vincennes, IN, and his father got a job as a sales manager for a gas company there.

Over the last few years, Custred told me recently, he began to feel that affirmative action was causing California to go through a process that reversed the journey of his youth: he saw it abandoning the amicable, everyone's-the-same racial climate that he believes characterized Indiana in the 50's and becoming as obsessed with racial classification as the pre-civil-rights South. In 1991, the legislature passed a bill (quickly vetoed by Governor Pete Wilson) that encouraged the state universities to strive for graduating classes that would reflect the state's ethnic makeup. Worse, there seemed to be no venue for complaints about such things. The press, it seemed to Custred, barely covered affirmative action. Five years ago, Custred came to the conclusion that an initiative would be the only way to get the issue on the public agenda. He began toying with wording he'd lifted straight from Lyndon B. Johnson's monument, the 1964 Civil Rights Act, and finally came up with this:

"Neither the State of California nor any of its political subdivisions or agents shall use race, sex, color, ethnicity, or national origin as a criterion for either discriminating against, or granting preferential treatment to, any individual or group in the operation of the state's system of public employment, public education or public contracting." That's almost an exact quote from the Civil Rights Act, except for the one little phrase about preferential treatment.

Suddenly, an Issue

To Glynn Custred, racial preference is a great injustice, the most significant departure from the principle of fairness in American social policy. To Patrick Chavis, affirmative action is the one opening into the system for people like him, generally consigned at birth to exist in a poor, self-enclosed black world. For Chavis, that feeling of race as destiny is the great unfairness in American life. Such perceptual stalemates can go on for many years, taking on an odd stability. But in 1995 that is no longer the case with regard to affirmative action. Mainly because of Custred and Wood's initiative, it has abruptly emerged as an issue that could decide the 1996 Presidential election. The country has to figure out who's right.

Custred and Wood were introduced by a mutual friend in 1991. For their first couple of years as a team, they had almost no luck in promoting their cause. Then, while driving home one day, Custred happened to hear William Rusher, the former publisher of *National Review*, on the radio. He gave Rusher a call and told him about the initiative, and Rusher wrote about it enthusiastically in his syndicated column. This led to the initiative's being taken up by the conservative press: William F. Buckley and Pat Buchanan praised it.

What changed everything, though, was the 1994 elections, which overnight transformed the abolition of affirmative action from a conservative-movement cause into a mainstream one. Three of the leading Republican presidential candidates, Bob

Dole, Phil Gramm, and Pete Wilson, all made statements opposing racial preference. (Earlier this month [June 1995], Wilson issued an executive order dismantling some of California's affirmative-action programs.) President Clinton publicly ordered up an internal review of affirmative action, something no previous President has done—which, at the very least, sent a signal of less-than-total commitment to affirmative action. A confidential report prepared for the President and obtained by the *Times* . . . seemed to be groping for some middle ground—backing the principle of affirmative action, criticizing some particular programs and expressing empathy for "bystanders," that is, white men. The President is expected to announce the result of his administration's review in a broad thematic speech . . . .

The issue cannot be an easy one for Clinton. He probably can't win re-election without carrying California, because the South has become so solidly Republican. Custred and Wood's initiative, which is overwhelmingly popular in early statewide polls, could have the effect of making the 1996 Presidential campaign in California a referendum on affirmative action: the California Civil Rights Initiative will probably face the voters on the same November day that Clinton does.

Earlier this spring, Clinton told the California state Democratic convention that he would countenance "no retreat" on affirmative action. But what he *didn't* do is come out against the initiative. If he does, he will have to sell California's voters on a position they don't like. However, if he endorses the initiative he will infuriate the Democratic base (in particular Willie Brown, the Speaker of the State Assembly). Thus, the initiative has gone, in a flash, from nowhere to the White House.

The Long, Liberal Silence

Beyond just the peculiar way the cards have fallen, there is an enormous well of pent-up hostility to affirmative action. The morally elegant vision of a color-blind society that Glynn Custred wrote into the initiative has the same animating power today that it did when used by the Reverend Dr. Martin Luther King Jr. in the 1960's. In addition, there is by now a vast trove of affirmative-action horror stories. Is there a white person who has never been told that the reason some desirable billet or other is unavailable is that it has been reserved for minorities under an affirmative-action program? Or who hasn't been privy to sorrowful, head-shaking conversation about this or that shockingly poor performance of black beneficiaries of affirmative action?

The opponents of affirmative action have been honing their arguments for a good thirty years. While the term and the programs associated with it embrace women and Hispanics, in politics and in the public mind affirmative action remains essentially a black-and-white issue. The opponents have learned not to make the argument too forcefully that affirmative action is unfair to white people. Instead, the anti-affirmative-action position now has prominent black spokesmen like Shelby Steele, the writer, and, in California, Ward Connerly, a member of the University of California Board of Regents. And the case is now built to a great extent on a rhetoric of what's good for blacks: affirmative action, opponents insist, does nothing to alleviate the worst problem in black America, the state of the poor ghettos. Instead, their argument goes, its beneficiaries are the best-off blacks, who, by being put above their academic or career level by affirmative action, are set up for failure in a way that damages their self-confidence and reinforces white prejudices about black inferiority.

A second essential anti-affirmative-action point that has come to the fore in recent years is that affirmative action is the opening wedge of a comprehensive ideology that threatens the basic American creed. If multiculturalism is given full sway, according to this argument, we'll find ourselves living in a society in which all decisions are made on the principle of apportionment to oppressed groups. "A lot of people use the word *Balkanization*," Glynn Custred says.

Arrayed against these compelling arguments is a very loud silence, especially from white liberals. Either opponents of affirmative action are patronizingly dismissed, as they were by President Clinton recently, as "angry white males" or they're told that they want to "turn back the clock" to the days before affirmative action, which opponents freely admit. The level of feeling among supporters of affirmative action, especially black ones, is obviously high, but the case for it is rarely laid out. It looks to the opponents as if there is some secret reason for affirmative action that liberals will not reveal—or no reason for it at all, in which case the supporters are merely people who are afraid of being yelled at by minorities.

As far as the public discourse goes, the next move is affirmative action's supporters to make. They need to acknowledge and confront the other side's position and then to explain why, nonetheless, America should still support affirmative-action programs.

Birth of a Concept

How did we get to this peculiar point? Whose idea was affirmative action in the first place? How did it spread? What does it actually consist of? And does it do any good?

The affirmative action trail begins faintly at the time of the Presidential inauguration of John F. Kennedy. At the Texas State Society's inaugural ball, Lyndon Johnson, the incoming Vice President, was pressing flesh in the receiving line. When a young black lawyer from Detroit named Hobart Taylor Jr.—known to Johnson because Hobart Taylor Sr., a businessman in Houston and an active Democrat, was a close friend—came through the line, Johnson pulled him aside and said he needed something. An executive order banning discriminatory hiring by Federal contractors was being drafted for President Kennedy's signature; could Taylor help work on it?

The next day, Taylor holed up in a room at the Willard Hotel with two future Supreme Court Justices, Arthur Goldberg and Abe Fortas, to prepare a document with the not-very-catchy title of Executive Order 10925. "I put the word *affirmative* in there at that time," Taylor later told an interviewer for the archives of the Lyndon Baines Johnson Library. "I was searching for something that would give a sense of positiveness to performance under that executive order, and I was torn between the words *positive action* and the words *affirmative action*. . . . And I took *affirmative action* because it was alliterative."

The key point about the inception of affirmative action is that it went virtually unnoticed. Executive Order 10925 merged two obscure Eisenhower administration committees that were supposed to prevent discriminatory hiring—one aimed at the civil service and the other at federal contractors—under the name of the President's Committee on Equal Employment Opportunity. The committee met 12 times. Its main activity was a program called "Plans for Progress," in which big federal contractors were persuaded to adopt voluntary efforts to increase their black employment.

Although the committee did not exercise much direct power and was not in the news, its basic mission clearly would offend present-day critics of affirmative action, since it was to promote race-conscious hiring. There wasn't any conservative backlash against the committee, because practically no one knew it existed. But as soon as President Kennedy proposed a civil rights bill in 1963, opponents began attacking it as one that would impose racial-quota hiring schemes. During the titanic Congressional debate that followed Johnson's proposing the Civil Rights Act in 1964, quotas were a frequent theme. "The bill would discriminate against white people," said Senator James Eastland of Mississippi. " . . . I know what will happen if the bill is passed. I know what will happen if there is a choice between hiring a white man or hiring a Negro both having equal qualifications. I know who will get the job. It will not be the white man."

The Civil Rights Act, therefore, contained a sentence explicitly disavowing quotas. And, although the law created an Equal Employment Opportunity Commission (EEOC) to prevent job discrimination, the commission was given no powers of enforcement whatsoever, so that it could not promote quota hiring; it was taking away the EEOC's enforcement power that prevented a Senate filibuster against the bill and so made its passage possible.

The passage of the Civil Rights Act set in motion a series of events that ended with President Johnson's issuing what is now regarded as the originating document of affirmative action: Executive Order 11246. Bear in mind what was on the minds of liberals at that time. Simply abolishing the South's legal apartheid system—the thrust of the Civil Rights Act—wasn't going to solve America's racial problems. There were small urban race riots in the summers of 1963 and 1964 and a large one in Watts in 1965. The gap between black and white was shockingly large. At the time, blacks were almost twice as likely as whites to be poor, twice as likely to be unemployed and more than four times as likely to be illiterate. The voices warning against quotas and reverse discrimination all seemed to belong to Southern segregationists, like Senators Eastland, Sam Ervin of North Carolina, Lister Hill of Alabama, J. William Fulbright of Arkansas and John Tower of Texas. So the anti-quota argument looked like merely a cover for something less legitimate.

The Invisible Milestone

The fullest expression of the liberal mood was a commencement address that President Johnson gave at Howard University on June 4, 1965. The key phrase (supplied by the young Daniel Patrick Moynihan) was, "We seek . . . not just equality as a right and a theory but equality as a fact and equality as a result." "Equality of result" has long been used by the opponents of affirmative action as the perfect distillation of the principle they find odious, but Johnson's speech was regarded within the White House as a great political triumph and the phrase generated no objections from the public.

Affirmative action specifically, however—the originating document, Executive Order 11246, issued on Sept. 24, 1965— appears to have been a kind of accident. The Civil Rights Act made the President's Committee on Equal Employment Opportunity, traditionally headed by the Vice President, potentially irrelevant, because it created several new government agencies to make sure blacks weren't being discriminated against. In February 1965, Johnson created a new President's Council on Equal Opportunity, to be headed by his vice president, Hubert Humphrey, a lifelong crusader for civil rights; this made Humphrey chairman of a White House committee and a White House council on the same thing.

Johnson ordered Humphrey to come up with a reorganization plan for all the government's civil rights organizations. Humphrey responded by proposing to abolish the equal opportunity committee but to keep alive the equal opportunity council. The council would be in charge of "community relations" (one of the new functions created by the Civil Rights Act) and of making sure federal contractors didn't discriminate against black job applicants—that is, affirmative action.

On June 21, 1965, shortly after his speech at Howard, Johnson approved this plan of Humphrey's. As late as mid-August, it was still on track. Then, in September, Johnson changed his mind. The reason is unknown, but it may have had to do with Humphrey's having made a hard-charging black lawyer named Wiley Branton the director of the equal opportunity council, which raised the possibility of controversial and high-profile civil rights enforcement actions emanating from the White House. A memo from a White House lawyer to Johnson, dated Sept. 20,

1965, lays out a scheme to abolish Humphrey's council entirely rather than give it more power. Community relations would be given to the Justice Department and affirmative action to a new Office of Federal Contract Compliance Programs in the Labor Department. "Humphrey can show his *bigness* by recommending the dissolution of a group that he heads which has performed its assignment and no longer needs to remain in existence," the memo said.

Humphrey's staff obediently drew up a memo to Johnson designed to make the official record reflect that the whole thing had been Humphrey's idea; Johnson's staff drew up a memo to Humphrey commending him for his statesmanship, and Executive Order 11246, which abolished the two White House equal opportunity groups and is now considered the opening bell for affirmative action, was drawn up and signed. There seemed to be two salient points about the executive order: it wasn't very important and it represented a setback for Hubert Humphrey and the civil rights cause because it did away with everything he headed. The *Times* first mentioned Executive Order 11246 three weeks after the fact, under the headline "Rights Groups Fear Easing of U.S. Enforcement Role." (By the way, Executive Order 11246 did not call for affirmative action to combat gender discrimination; that was added a few years later after prodding by feminist groups. The original concept of affirmative action was exclusively racial.)

The reason that Executive Order 11246 did, in fact, turn out to be a milestone is that it took affirmative action out of the White House, which is under intense perpetual scrutiny and has a small staff with high turnover, and made it the raison d'être of a division of the Labor Department. This meant there would be a much larger and more permanent staff devoted to carrying out affirmative action—a staff with the power to write federal regulations and with the maneuvering room that comes from the press not reporting on your every move.

Because the end of segregation came in the form of a bill being passed, the country realized it was making a momentous change. The Civil Rights Act of 1964 was furiously debated and examined. Compromises were struck. The result was that by the time the act became law, Americans had consciously made up their minds to take this great step. Executive Order 11246 had exactly the opposite dynamic: it was an invisible milestone that was not debated at all (or noticed, even) before the fact. Given its significance, it was inevitable that it would be publicly debated with Civil Rights Act-like intensity at some point after the fact—and now we are at that point.

The Meritocracy as a Racial Barrier

The original, executive-order definition of affirmative action is that it requires employers only to search aggressively for qualified minority applicants—through advertising, for instance, or special recruitment efforts. Once found, these new minority applicants would go into the same pool with everybody else and the final selection would be made on a color-blind basis. Almost everybody, including the leading critics of affirmative action and the majority of respondents in polls, claims to support affirmative action if we could stick to the original definition, and most defenders of affirmative action say that it's only the official definition that they're defending.

But there's an enormous problem with putting the official definition into practice. The civil rights revolution occurred at the same time that an even more important change in American society was taking place: the construction—by liberals, it should be noted—of a formal meritocracy based on education and standardized testing. This country has always been obsessed with individual opportunity, but before the 1950's there was no system in place that could evaluate and assign a numerical value to every American. At the time that affirmative action began, there was such a system and it judged people mainly on a single criterion, their ability to get good grades in school. (Most standardized tests are designed to predict school grades.)

In a way, the construction of this meritocratic system was good for the civil rights movement because it provided a target to aim at. It's no accident that the string of landmark cases leading to *Brown v. Board of Education* involved schools; it was the argument that education equals opportunity that dealt the death blow to legal segregation. But in a crucial sense, the numerical, education-based meritocracy was bad news for blacks. It rendered the key affirmative-action concept of creating biracial pools of equally qualified applicants meaningless, because now everybody was ranked serially. And it apportioned opportunity on the basis of performance in the one area where blacks were most disadvantaged: education. For as long as there have been standardized tests, blacks have on average scored lower than whites. As education for blacks has improved, the gap has closed substantially and is now at an all-time low, but it is still large enough that for institutions, hiring and admitting purely on the basis of educational credentials would produce extremely low counts of blacks, and also of Latinos and American Indians. To cite just one example, in 1992 only 1,493 African Americans had SAT verbal scores of 600 or above—and 55,224 whites.

The history of affirmative action can be seen as a struggle over the fairness of the modern meritocracy, with minorities arguing that educational measures shouldn't be the deciding factor in who gets ahead and opponents of affirmative action saying that to bend the criteria for blacks is to discriminate unfairly against more deserving whites. The 1964 Civil Rights Act contained an amendment put in by John Tower explicitly permitting the use of standardized tests in hiring. However, the first few important Supreme Court cases on affirmative action—in particular *Griggs v. Duke Power Company* in 1971—went in the opposite, pro-minority, direction by restricting the use of test scores as screens for employment. (The Court has swung the other way more recently.) Either way, the trade-off is stark and will remain so until black America and white America are on the same educational and cultural footing—in other words, for generations. If hiring and admission are done purely on the basis of test scores, the black presence will be a fraction of what it is in the population, and bringing it higher requires rejecting some whites who scored better than the blacks who were hired or admitted.

What present-day opponents of affirmative action, smelling victory, don't like to admit is that these are issues capable of generating real confusion in the minds of people of good will. An education-based meritocracy makes its judgments about people before they've ever really done anything, based on a measure, school performance, that depends heavily on who their parents are and what kind of environment they create. People tend to shy away from meritocracy in pure form, or at least to want to sand off its rough edges, because the definition of merit seems too narrow and because it doesn't seem genuinely to offer equal opportunity to everyone. No American institution of higher education is willing to select solely on the basis of (as opposed to mainly on the basis of) merit as defined by grades and test scores.

The Justice Who Couldn't Make Up His Mind

The Supreme Court's *Griggs* decision left a perfect opening for a case filed by a white student who felt he'd been discriminated against in higher-education admissions. It was one thing to limit the use of educational credentials in hiring, but it would seem absurd to do so in admission to a school—even though it was precisely by departing from strict adherence to educational credentials that majority-white schools were able to register a large increase in black students during the late 1960s and early 1970s.

Robert Klitgaard, a social scientist, calculated that in one year in the 1970s, if affirmative action had been eliminated, the total number of blacks in law school in America would have dropped from 1,539 to 285—which presumably meant that the total number of whites would have risen by the same number. In 1971, one of these discriminated-against whites sued: Marco DeFunis, who had been rejected by the University of Washington law school even though his grades and test scores put him ahead of virtually all the black students who were accepted.

DeFunis won his case and entered the law school under a court order. The Washington State Supreme Court reversed the decision and ordered him out. DeFunis appealed to the United States Supreme Court, which stayed the lower-court decision, permitting him to remain, and agreed to hear the case. The Justice who wrote the order keeping DeFunis in law school was William O. Douglas, the longest-serving member of the Supreme Court in American history. Douglas's papers, which have been opened, provide an extraordinary (and heretofore unknown) look at a strong mind blowing its fuses over affirmative action.

Douglas, then seventy-five years old and the last of Franklin Roosevelt's appointees remaining on the Court, was himself the product of humble origins in the state of Washington; his own meteoric rise had been set off by admission to law school. He had every reason to empathize with Marco DeFunis. At the same time, he was a fiery liberal and champion of the downtrodden who had come down on the side of blacks in every landmark civil rights case.

One of Douglas's clerks, Ira Ellman, wrote him a memo recommending that he vote for the Court to take up the case because "there really was some kind of quota here," which he thought was a wrong that ought to be corrected. The Court did grant DeFunis a hearing and then recessed; in March 1974, with DeFunis only weeks away from his law-school graduation, the justices began working on their opinions again. It quickly became apparent that Douglas would be the swing vote: four justices wanted to kick De-Funis out of law school while four wanted to order his admission.

Douglas was known within the Supreme Court building as someone who made up his mind about every case instantly and then quickly dashed off an opinion. He had little use for lengthy colloquy or deliberation with his clerks, who barely saw him. But in the case of DeFunis, uncharacteristically, he seemed genuinely torn. Ellman, sensing that Douglas couldn't make up his mind, hesitantly offered to draft an opinion himself—something Douglas's clerks never did. Douglas told Ellman to go ahead, as long as he didn't circulate the draft to the other justices.

"I don't know about these tests," Douglas told Ellman by way of instruction—meaning the Law School Aptitude Test (LSAT). What he was getting at was that perhaps the way to a liberal opinion lay through pointing out that the test (which hadn't existed back in Douglas's law-student days) was biased against blacks. Before putting Ellman in charge of the opinion, Douglas had dashed off some wording, dated March 8, 1974, that said the LSAT was "by no means objective" and might contain "hidden bias." Ellman obtained data from the Educational Testing Service, however, showing that the LSAT did not inaccurately predict blacks' grades.

Douglas's early wording strongly opposed reverse discrimination. "The democratic ideal as I read the Constitution and Bill of Rights presupposes an aristocracy of talent, and all races must be permitted to compete for a position in that hierarchy," it said. How, then, to square the circle? Douglas proposed that the law school first admit "those clearly qualified" purely on academic merit and then fill the rest of its places by a lottery.

On March 11, the justices decided privately to declare the case moot. The stated reason was that DeFunis was about to graduate (today he's practicing law in Seattle) and the underlying reason was that no clear majority position on the issue was emerging. But Douglas decided to steam ahead and produce a dissent that would address the merits of the case; as he told Ellman, "I might not be around next time this issue comes up."

On March 21, there was another draft of Douglas's opinion. This one argued that the school should be allowed to admit minorities with lower test scores than whites who were rejected. But the very next day, there was another draft taking a different position: that while "racial classifications cannot be used," universities should discriminate in favor of people from disadvantaged backgrounds.

The following draft, printed up a few days later, showed that Douglas's opposition to racial preferences was becoming firmer. But Douglas still couldn't accept the idea of the law school's admitting people purely on the basis of academic credentials. Another draft was produced, which said, "The presence of an LSAT test is sufficient warrant for a school to separate minorities into a class in order better to probe their capacities and potentials."

Douglas ordered Ellman to circulate this draft to the other justices. But the next morning, he called Ellman into his office and said, matter-of-factly rather than accusingly, that he actually hadn't wanted the draft circulated, so Ellman should go and retrieve all the copies from the justices' offices. When Ellman came back with them, Douglas told him that from now on he would work on the opinion without any help.

He then wrote one last draft: this time, rather than coming down on one or another side of the case, he came down on both at the same time. He was strongly against reverse discrimination, but insisted that DeFunis had not been discriminated against on the basis of his race when he was denied admission. So, for the first time in all the drafts, he did not order DeFunis admitted to law school. When the Supreme Court printer delivered the opinion to Ira Ellman he said, with a quizzical look, "He changed the bottom line."

The way Douglas got to this final position was by returning to his attack on the LSAT, with greater fury than ever before. It is racially biased, he wrote; its bias justifies reverse bias by the law school; in fact, the LSAT should be abolished entirely. That Douglas decided to declare the LSAT biased although he had no evidence that it was is mainly a demonstration that he was intellectually trapped and couldn't find any other way out. He couldn't reconcile his passionate belief in meritocracy with the actual meritocracy's mechanical feeling and its tendency to reward some ethnic cultures far more than others. So he went through every possible feeling one can have about affirmative action in sequence and wound up in effect throwing up his hands.

A year later, Justice Douglas had a stroke and retired from the Court. In 1977, a case almost exactly like that of DeFunis presented itself to the Court: *Bakke v. Regents of the University of California*. The University of California-Davis Medical School had created a separate admissions pool for minority applicants and rejected higher-ranked white applicants to make room for them. One of these was Allan Bakke.

Douglas's seat on the Court had been taken by John Paul Stevens, but his position as swing vote had been assumed by Lewis F. Powell, a gentlemanly former corporate lawyer with none of Douglas's Whitmanesque pretensions. Powell, unlike Douglas, found a logical route to a decision, but it would be difficult to find a less resounding one on a major issue in the history of the Supreme Court. By a 5–4 majority, the Court struck down U.C.-Davis's racial-quota admissions system and ordered Bakke admitted. Also by a 5–4 majority, however, with Powell on the other side this time, the Court approved the idea of taking race into account as a positive factor in admissions decisions, in order to achieve a diverse student body. The decision may have been a statesmanlike piece of jurisprudence, but in admissions-office circles it is widely viewed as meaning that it's OK to reverse discriminate as long as you're not really obvious about it.

The Establishment Embraces Affirmative Action

Much of what is now most unpopular about affirmative action occurred well after the heyday of civil rights. The two small federal affirmative-action bureaucracies established in 1965—the Equal Employment Opportunity Commission and the Office of Federal Contract Compliance—both defined their mission as being to promote affirmative action aggressively. They quickly began to deal with companies in terms of numerical racial hiring "goals."

"The average business guy wants to know what to do," Edward Sylvester, who was the first head of the contract compliance office, told me recently. "You've got to give him numbers. They'd say, 'Tell me what you want and when.'"

Richard Nixon and George Shultz, when he was Secretary of Labor, imposed the government's harshest, most explicit quota plan ever on building contractors in Philadelphia in 1969; we now know from the diaries and notes of John Ehrlichman and H. R.

Haldeman that Nixon thought of the Philadelphia Plan as a wonderful way to pit two key Democratic constituencies, blacks and labor, against each other and endorsed it partly for that reason.

. . . Last year's [1995] poster child in reverse for affirmative action is Frank Washington, the black millionaire who tried to use the Federal Communications Commission's (FCC) minority tax certificate program (known in the trade as "Section 1071") in order to make a quick killing for himself and a white billionaire, Sumner Redstone of Viacom. Section 1071 began during the Carter Administration and was expanded during the Reagan administration. The contract office's current regulations—41 Code of Federal Regulations 60.2—contain such notorious provisions as a requirement that "effective affirmative-action programs" must include "active support of local and national community action programs and community service programs"—that is, mandated charity. They were promulgated in 1978 under Jimmy Carter. So were federal minority set-asides for federal contractors. "Race-norming," the practice (later outlawed) of not directly comparing the test scores of white and black applicants for federal employment, was begun in 1980.

Through the years, states and localities by the dozens were creating affirmative-action laws of their own. And even more significant than whatever government has done has been the massive and largely voluntary adoption of affirmative-action plans by virtually all big institutions. The current conversational meaning of affirmative action is something like "stuff that's done explicitly to help black people"—the stuff being everything from preferential college admissions to the way news is covered to what's hung in museums to corporate promotion practices. All of this followed from the civil rights movement and President Johnson's embrace of it, but it isn't explicitly attributable to the exercise of federal power.

Part of what was propelling affirmative action was that it had an interest group behind it, namely minority organizations. Much of their support of affirmative action is standard political behavior. Black people don't control America, though. All along, the overwhelmingly white establishment has supported affirmative action and that is what accounts for its durability. The establishment's reasoning, never openly stated, would have gone something like this: Sure, affirmative action generates white victims of reverse discrimination, but there aren't very many of them and they don't suffer too greatly. They go to Colgate instead of Cornell. Big deal. The most clearly outstanding whites—the people the meritocracy set up to spot and train for leadership—don't suffer at all. In return, we are able to take some of the edge off of what has been the most explosive issue in our history, the one that set off our bloodiest war and our worst civil disturbances. We create an integrated authority system. We give blacks a stake. It promotes the peace. In addition, case by case, it creates a feeling of doing something to correct our worst historic wrong.

All through the 1970's and 1980's, this quiet but firm establishment support for affirmative action worked to quell incipient revolts against it. Richard Nixon campaigned against quotas and then did not abolish affirmative action. So did Ronald Reagan and so did George Bush.

The closest that affirmative action came to being done away with during the Reagan-Bush years was in 1985, after Reagan was overwhelmingly re-elected and the confrontational Donald Regan succeeded James Baker as the White House chief of staff. A group of conservative officials, including Edwin Meese, W. Bradford Reynolds, the Assistant Attorney General for Civil Rights, and William Bennett, had been talking for years about replacing Executive Order 11246 with something similar to the California Civil Rights Initiative. In the second term, they decided to renew the push. Their problem was that in early 1985 Raymond Donovan, the Secretary of Labor and a fellow movement conservative, had resigned and been replaced by Bill Brock, a moderate who wanted to protect the Office of Federal Contract Compliance.

The anti-affirmative-action group made the mistake of overplaying its hand. While Brock was away on a lengthy foreign trip, they presented their idea to Reagan, who seemed interested. But Donald Regan felt that he and Brock were being circumvented and put a stop to it. The attempt on the life of Executive Order 11246 was leaked to the press and the resulting outcry saved the executive order.

"The internal argument was, 'We're expending a lot of political capital on this issue.'" Reynolds recalled not long ago. "'It's getting in the way of other things that are more important. The less problems for Reagan the better. Let's don't carry this further now. We can always revisit it later.'"

Soon afterward, Reagan nominated Reynolds to be Associate Attorney General and, after a rough hearing, the Senate Judiciary Committee refused to recommend him for the position because of his opposition to affirmative action. In 1990, C. Boyden Gray, an aide to President Bush, tried to get Bush to sign an executive order banning racial preferences in employment; again, there was a leak to the press followed by a backing down. In 1991, an Assistant Secretary of Education named Michael Williams announced that the government would be eliminating scholarships that were reserved for black students only. After another immediate controversy, Bush reversed the policy.

These public disputes aside, the reigning assumption of elected officialdom, including Republican officialdom, was pro-affirmative action. Bob Dole has recently come out against preferences, but for many years he supported it. When she was Secretary of Labor, Elizabeth Dole held a ceremony to celebrate the 25th anniversary of Executive Order 11246 and presented a plaque to Edward Sylvester, the first head of the contract office. Ten years ago, while working on a magazine profile of Newt Gingrich, I watched him work hard to get gate assignments at the Atlanta airport for a new airline, for the sole reason that its founder was black. Then he called the White House and suggested that Reagan mention this in his inaugural address. Such behavior by a rising leader of the Republican right was completely unremarkable at the time.

The establishment clearly believed that affirmative action had become a permanent part of the American landscape. There was a steady diet of Supreme Court cases; university administrators and corporate officials kept modifying and fine-tuning their programs. What the establishment didn't quite grasp was how bad affirmative action looked from the outside—the way it seemed all-pervasive and undemocratic. A review that Senator Dole recently ordered up from the Library of Congress found that there are 162 separate federal affirmative-action programs, and that leaves out all the state, local and private ones.

It's arguable that there wasn't a single law passed in Congress that truly endorsed the broad principle of affirmative action until the Civil Rights Act of 1991. Way back in the 1960s, liberals got used to the idea that you could never get Congress to do the right thing on racial matters, so the way to make public policy was through the judicial and executive branches. These were the venues through which affirmative action was pursued. So down through the decades, the muscles that liberals would have used to make a public case for affirmative action atrophied—and the conservatives' were becoming magnificently buffed and toned. What's good about the current crisis for affirmative action is that it means a debate will take place that should have taken place long ago; if it had, affirmative action wouldn't be so vulnerable now.

The Case for Affirmative Action

What would the country look like without affirmative action? According to its opponents, a gentle notching downward would take place in black America: black students who now go to Harvard Law School would go to Michigan instead and do very well; black students at Michigan would go to Louisiana State, and so on. The net impact would be small. And maybe then we would get to work on the real issues, like the poor quality of many all-black urban public schools.

The other possibility is that there would be an enormous decrease in black representation everywhere in white-collar (and also blue-collar) America, with a big, noticeable depressive effect on black income, employment, home-ownership and education levels. The percentage of blacks in managerial and technical jobs doubled during the affirmative action years. During the same period, as Andrew Hacker pointed out in his book *Two Nations*, the number of black police officers rose from 24,000 to 64,000 and the number of black electricians from 14,000 to 43,000. If affirmative action were entirely abolished, does anyone really believe the government would undertake, say, an expensive upgrade of education for blacks as a more meaningful substitute?

Black America is still a substantially separate world. Blacks are by far the most residentially segregated ethnic group and the least likely to intermarry. Without affirmative action, the gap would surely become even more pronounced. The lack of faith in the fairness of the system that is so much more a part of the black world than the white would only increase.

The goal of affirmative action is not to reject the spirit of integration in favor of race-consciousness but to bring blacks into the mainstream of national life. The ironic result of affirmative action being abolished could be an increase, not a decrease, in the kind of black demands for reparations and mandated percentages of the action that whites find so annoying: if you're out of the system completely, then you don't seek access to jobs and school places. You just want more resources.

The opponents tend to treat affirmative action as a unitary evil: all the many varieties are equally wrong and disastrous, and the most extreme Frank Washington-type excesses are a fair representation of the totality of the phenomenon. In fact, the country is full of affirmative-action plans that work pretty well and affirmative-action beneficiaries whom people like. Clifford Alexander, who was head of the Equal Employment Opportunity Commission, was Secretary of the Army in the Carter administration; he says that the first time a list of people being promoted to general landed on his desk, he sent it back, demanding that more good black candidates be found. One of these was Colin Powell, who recently departed from his usual sphinx-like silence on public issues to make a speech defending affirmative action. In California, the psychic center of the affirmative-action debate is undergraduate admissions to Berkeley; the initiative literature uses the statistic that "the dropout rate for students admitted under affirmative-action programs often runs as high as 75 percent." According to the university, 60 percent of its black students (there are only about two hundred in each class of three thousand, by the way) graduate within six years, as against 84 percent of white students. Rather than Berkeley cruelly taking its black students up past their *level*, it has a black graduation rate 50 percent higher than the national average.

It's entirely possible, indeed likely, that the more egregious forms of affirmative action can be jettisoned. This is already happening: the notorious FCC minority tax certificate program was legislatively abolished . . . . As we begin the process of thinking about the remaining bulk of affirmative-action programs, it's important to keep in mind three core principles.

First, because the country is so segregated, the natural default position for white people is to have no contact at all with blacks. It's healthy to have some way of pushing people, as they make hiring and contracting and admissions decisions, to go far enough past the bounds of their ordinary realm of contacts to find black candidates. Even the opponents say they want this, but it won't happen if it's not required because the black-white social gulf is so great.

Second, lawsuits and regulations are not the ideal venue for affirmative action. Liberal victories won there tend to be Pyrrhic: they generate enormous public resentment that leads to their eventual demise and gives the whole cause of trying to improve race relations a bad name. A legislation-based affirmative action would perforce be one that was spiritedly debated publicly. Liberals would have to make their case in a way that would convince people, and the result would be compromised-over programs with sustainable public support.

Third, we should recognize that the meritocracy is structured in such a way that one criterion, educational performance, is overweighted and has become too much the sole path to good jobs and leadership positions. It shows how far we've gone in this direction, how much we accept the present social arrangement as the natural order of things, that affirmative-action plans governing school admissions and entry-level hiring for twenty-two-year-olds are so often criticized as constituting "equality of result." Rationally, a first job or a place in school is an opportunity; it's only because we sort people so firmly so early that it looks like a result. There is a real difference between affirmative-action plans that seek to divide up the spoils and plans that seek to get African Americans into a position where they have a chance to prove themselves through individual performance.

Every child born in America doesn't have access to good schools and doesn't have parents who encourage study. Many blacks go to the worst schools and live in the toughest family circumstances. To argue that by late adolescence black people have run a fair competitive race and that if they're behind whites on the educational standards they deserve to be permanently barred from the professional and managerial classes is absurd. It constitutes not just a denial of opportunity to individuals but a denial of talent to the society.

The Case Of Dr. Chavis

Allan Bakke, after graduating from medical school, did his residency at the Mayo Clinic in Minnesota. Today he is an anesthesiologist in Rochester, MN. Bakke doesn't speak to the press and he didn't respond to my request for an interview. He does not appear to have set the world on fire as a doctor. He has no private practice and works on an interim basis, rather than as a staff physician, at Olmsted Community Hospital.

Patrick Chavis, who took Allan Bakke's place at U.C.-Davis med school, fits the stereotype of the affirmative-action beneficiary in one way: as he freely admits, he would not have been admitted strictly on the basis of his grades and test scores, though they were good. In other ways, though, he does not fit. He is not a product of the cushy black upper class: he grew up in South Central Los Angeles, the eldest of five children of a welfare mother who had migrated to California from rural Arkansas. Chavis first met his father three years ago, when he was 40. One day when he was in high school, one of his teachers used the word "indigents" in class. That night, upset, he asked his mother if that word meant people like them. "Who else do you think it means?" she asked him.

Another way in which Patrick Chavis doesn't fit the stereotype of the affirmative-action beneficiary is that he doesn't give the impression of being tormented by self-doubt over whether he really deserves to be where he is. If anything, he seems to assume a superiority over his white medical-school classmates. He says he works harder than they do and in tougher conditions. He and his four black classmates set up a primary-care clinic when they were at Davis and worked there as volunteers, but they couldn't get any of the white students to join them. While he was still a resident at the University of Southern California, he and one of his black classmates from Davis each put up $500 and opened a small practice, so that they could "hit the ground running" when they graduated. He ticks off what the black doctors admitted under Davis's special minorities-only program (which was eliminated after the Supreme Court's *Bakke* decision, resulting in subsequent classes having only one or two black members) are doing now: almost all are in primary care in underserved areas, including his ex-wife, Toni Johnson Chavis, a pediatrician in Compton. If Chavis hadn't gotten into medical school, his patients wouldn't be treated by some better-qualified white obstetrician; they'd have no doctor at all and their babies would be delivered the way Chavis was—by whoever happened to be on duty at the emergency room of the county hospital.

Rather than believing that if it weren't for affirmative action he would be functioning in a color-blind environment, Chavis sees the old-fashioned kind of racial discrimination everywhere. The idea that, as an obstetrician-gynecologist, he could build a practice on the west side of Los Angeles based on middle-class white women is a joke. The Bank of America wouldn't lend him the money to build his house because it is in a rundown black neighborhood. He has staff privileges at St. Francis Hospital in

Lynwood, where all the obstetricians are black or Latino, but got into a fiery dispute with Long Beach Memorial Medical Center, where for a while he was the only black OB admitting patients. The hospital put him under professional review, saying he had performed a substandard delivery. Chavis felt the real issue was that the hospital didn't want him admitting Medicaid patients. He sued the hospital for discrimination and won—but the judge overturned the verdict; she mentioned that the jury's award of $1.1 million in damages seemed unwarranted, since he bills Medicaid $800,000 a year. Rather than feeling sheepish about making so much money, Chavis points out that Medical reimburses at the rate of $14 per office visit and $400 per vaginal delivery. His white classmates, with their higher-paying privately insured patients, do fewer deliveries and make more. He has been audited by the state and by the Internal Revenue Service, which he does not attribute to bad luck. "We do it with enthusiasm and with joy, and we fight the system," he says.

So Patrick Chavis fiercely defends affirmative action and holds himself up as an example of the good that it does. "There's no way in hell—if it wasn't for some kind of affirmative action, there wouldn't be any black doctors," he says. "Maybe one or two. Things haven't changed that much."

BIBLIOGRAPHY

An asterisk (*) preceding a reference indicates that the article or part of it has been reprinted in this book.

BOOKS AND PAMPHLETS

Altschiller, Donald, ed. Affirmative action. H. W. Wilson. '91.

Belz, Herman. Equality transformed: a quarter-century of affirmative action. Transaction. '91.

Blank, Renee & Slipp, Sandra. Voices of diversity: real people talk about problems and solutions in a workplace where everyone is not alike. Amacom. '94.

Boxer, Barbara & Boxer, Nicole. Strangers in the Senate: politics and the new revolution of women in America. National. '94.

Brimmer, Andrew F. & Simms, Margaret C. Economic perspectives on affirmative action. Joint Center for Political & Economic Studies. '95.

Cahn, Steven M. Affirmative action and the university. Temple University Press. '93.

Carter, Stephen L. Reflections of an affirmative action baby. Basic. '91.

Clayton, Susan D. & Crosby, Faye J. Justice, gender, and affirmative action. University of Michigan Press. '92.

De Freitas, Gregory. Inequality at work: Hispanics in the U.S. labor force. Oxford University Press. '91.

D'Souza, Dinesh. Illiberal education: the politics of race and sex on campus. Vintage. '92.

Edwards, Audrey & Polite, Craig. Children of the dream. Doubleday. '92.

Ezorsky, Gertrude. Racism and justice: the case for affirmative action. Cornell University Press. '91.

Felkenes, George T. & Unsinger, Peter Charles, eds. Diversity, affirmative action, and law enforcement. Thomas. '92.

Fernandez, John P. Managing a diverse work force. Lexington. '91.

Fix, Michael & Struyk, Raymond J., eds. Clear and convincing evidence: measurement of discrimination in America. Urban Institute Press. '93.

Gardenswartz, Lee & Rowe, Anita. Managing diversity. Pfeiffer. '93.

Hanmer, Trudy J. Affirmative action: opportunity for all? Enslow. '93.

Harrigan, John J. Empty dreams, empty pockets: class and bias in American politics. Macmillan. '93.

Harrison, Maureen & Gilbert, Steve, eds. Landmark decisions of the United States Supreme Court. Excellent. '91.

Jackson, Susan E. et al. Diversity in the workplace. Guildford. '92.

Jamieson, David & O'Mara, Julie. Managing workplace 2000: gaining the diversity advantage. Jossey-Bass. '91.

Keating, W. Dennis. The suburban housing dilemma. Temple University Press. '94.

Kirp, David L. et al. Our town: race, housing, and the soul of suburbia. Rutgers University Press. '95.

Knouse, Stephen B. et al. Hispanics in the workplace. Sage. '92.

Loden, Marilyn & Rosener, Judy. Workforce America! Managing employee diversity as a vital resource. Irwin. '91.

McNaught, Brian. Gay issues in the workplace. St. Martin's. '93.

Mills, Nicolaus, ed. Debating affirmative action: race, gender, ethnicity, and the politics of inclusion. Delta. '94.

Morrison, Ann M. The new leaders: guidelines on leadership diversity in America. Jossey-Bass. '92.

Nieli, Russell. Racial preference and racial justice: the new affirmative action controversy. Ethics & Public Policy Center. '91.

Orlans, Harold & O'Neill, June, eds. Affirmative action revisited. Sage. '92.

Palmer, Ezra. Everything you need to know about discrimination. Rosen. '90.

Querry, Ronald B. Native American struggle for equality. Rourke. '92.

Rivera, Miquela. The minority career book. Bab Adams, Inc. '91.

Roberts, Celia, Jupp, T. C. & Davis, Evelyn. Language and discrimination: a study of communication in multiethnic workplaces. Longman. '92.

Robertson, Nan. The girls in the balcony: women, men, and the New York Times. Random. '92.

Rosenfeld, Michel. Affirmative action and justice: a philosophical and constitutional inquiry. Yale University Press. '91.

Rothenberg, Paula S. Race, class, and gender. St. Martin's. '92.

Samuels, Suzanne. Fetal rights, women's rights: gender and equality in the workplace. University of Wisconsin Press. '95.

Shapiro, Joseph. No pity: people with disabilities forging a new civil rights movement. Times. '93.

Shorris, Earl. Latinos. Norton. '92.

Sniderman, Paul M. et al. Prejudice, politics, and the American dilemma. Stanford University Press. '93.

Sowell, Thomas. Preferential policies: an international prospective. Morrow. '90.

Spiegel, Fredelle Z. Women's wages, women's worth. Continuum. '94.

Steele, S. The content of our characters: a new vision of race in America. St. Martin's. '90.

Takagi, Dana Y. The retreat from race: Asian-American admissions and racial politics. Rutgers University Press. '92.

Taylor, Bron Raymond. Affirmative action at work. University of Pittsburgh. '91.

Terkel, Studs. Race. New. '92.

Thomas, R. Roosevelt. Beyond race and gender. Amacom. '91.

United States Commission on Civil Rights. Civil rights issues facing Asian Americans. U.S. Government Printing Office. '92.

Urofsky, Melvin I. A conflict of rights: the Supreme Court and affirmative action. Scribner's. '91.

Vianello, Mino & Siemienska, Renata. Gender inequality: a comparative study of discrimination and participation. Sage. '90.

ADDITIONAL PERIODICAL ARTICLES WITH ABSTRACTS

For those who wish to read more widely on the subject of affirmative action, this section contains abstracts of additional articles that bear on the topic. Readers who require a comprehensive list of materials are advised to consult the *Readers' Guide to Periodical Literature* and other Wilson indexes.

Affirmative reactions. Robert F. Drinan. *America* 172:4–5 Ap 1 '95

A backlash is growing against affirmative action in the United States. Opponents maintain that the effectiveness of affirmative action programs has come to an end. Arguing that this generation should not be required to do reparation for the evils of the past, they protest "discrimination in reverse." In fact, every generation of Americans has been required to pay taxes for the mistakes of the past. Moreover, affirmative action has helped produce notable improvements for African Americans, women, and Hispanics.

The color of California. Jeremy A. Rabkin. *The American Spectator* 28:24–7 My '95

The Supreme Court has not been friendly to voter initiatives in the past. In cases such as *Hunter v. Erickson*, *Reitman v. Mulkey*, and *Washington v. Seattle School District*, the Court overturned popular voter initiatives, arguing that they were unconstitutional. This trend does not bode well for the California Civil Rights Initiative, a proposal to prohibit the state government from imposing preferences based on race, sex, or ethnicity in higher education admissions, government employment, and government contract awards. According to early opinion polls, there is overwhelming public support for the initiative. Thus far, the Court has been able to get away with its dismissals of voters' demands because an entrenched liberal majority in Congress shared its views, but the new Republican Congress could challenge the Court.

Affirmative on affirmative action. Don Wycliff. *Commonweal* 122:11-2 My 19 '95

The era of affirmative action seems to be coming to a close. One of the problems with affirmative action is the doubt it has planted within the community of people it was intended to help. More troubling, however, has been the expansion of groups and categories who are counted as "excluded" or "disadvantaged" and qualify as beneficiaries of a policy that was designed exclusively for African Americans and Native Americans. Affirmative action has not only lost support but has inspired opposition and anger as well. Though opponents' complaints are overblown, not much can be done to restore the sense of compensatory justice on which affirmative action depends. For blacks, the loss will be more symbolic than substantive as long as the true spirit of affirmative action is not allowed to expire.

Action still needed. *Commonweal* 122:3-4 Je 2 '95

There may be problems with affirmative action, but now is not the time to dismantle it. Affirmative action policies have been critical to the national effort to compensate for the injustices visited upon African Americans for centuries, but they have not, as some say, given blacks a free ride or resulted in reverse discrimination. The current debate over affirmative action should focus on establishing a set of guidelines on educational achievement, employment rates, median income, and residential integration that would signal the final redress of a national injustice.

Jesse Jackson urges young blacks to unite to fight for affirmative action. *Jet* 88:10 Jl 10 '95

In what he calls an attempt to fan the flames of 1960s activism, Jesse Jackson recently urged young blacks to take up the cause of affirmative action, which has come under attack by the United States Supreme Court. Jackson blames the recent backlash against affirmative action on a shifting job market and a lack of leadership.

In defence of affirmative action. Fred Bruning. *Maclean's* 108:9 Mr 20 '95

Affirmative action has not allowed minorities to hit the jackpot at the expense of white American males, as some people believe. This belief is a fantasy fed by politicians trying to win votes, right-wing radio clowns, and even some liberals who say that affirmative action has outlived its usefulness. If white males really believe that it is great to be black in America, they should move to the other side of the tracks and report back in six months.

A white male backlash. Carl Mollins. *Maclean's* 108:22-3 Mr 20 '95

A backlash is growing against affirmative action in the United States. Described by President Clinton as "a leg up" for women, blacks, Hispanics, and native Americans, U.S. affirmative action incentives and regulations require federally funded educators and employers to give women and racial minorities a fair chance at career success. Republican legislators are spearheading a charge to undo or amend thirty years of affirmative action law, which they claim constitutes reverse discrimination against white males. Despite a plea by Clinton to insulate affirmative action from partisan politics, many analysts conclude that the issue will loom large over the 1996 presidential election.

Coastal sounding. David Corn. *The Nation* 260:405-6 Mr 27 '95

A California anti-affirmative action initiative—likely to be on the ballot next year—could determine the outcome of the 1996 race for the presidency. The Clinton White House cannot afford to make a serious mistake in its handling of the issue: The initiative will likely draw voters to the polls who are not sympathetic to President Clinton, and without a victory in California in 1996, he could lose the election. In his first press conference of the Gingrich era, Clinton flubbed questions on affirmative action, wandering all over the map with contradictory statements. The challenge for Clinton is to shape a coherent message on the issue. The article discusses the pro-affirmative action views of Jesse Jackson.

Beyond misery. JoAnn Wypijewski. *The Nation* 260:439-40 Ap 3 '95

Those on the left should not accept the evasive debate on the future of welfare and affirmative action but should address the real problems. Affirmative action, welfare, and all the tinkerings of the Great Society were efforts to manage misery while evading the trickier problems of racism, inequality, and exploitation that caused the misery in the first place. While the economy was expanding, the measures worked well enough, but with bad times, the programs are easy targets. Neither Gingrich nor Clinton has anything to say about the state of affairs that has seen only the top 20 percent of the population increase their real income over the past fifteen years. Both politicians govern for the top slice and are happy to distract the rest with a fight over society's crumbs. The left should debate the distribution of power and income, work and its fetishization, and the true interests of people and the possibility for happiness and democracy.

Subject to debate. Katha Pollitt. *The Nation* 260:552 Ap 24 '95

Pundits spouting the anti-affirmative action phrase "equality of opportunity, not equality of result" may not know what they are really asking for. It is unlikely that those who find affirmative action too burdensome, costly, intrusive, and unfair would prefer the sweeping measures needed to even begin to equalize opportunity for all Americans regardless of race, gender, or ethnicity. To eliminate the opportunity-killing effects of poverty, it would be necessary to eradicate poverty itself.

Hiring quotas for white males only. Eric Foner. *The Nation* 260:92–4+ Je 26 '95

The debate over affirmative action, the latest "wedge" issue in American politics, reflects a disturbing lack of historical perspective. The U.S. has never operated on a color-blind basis. Slavery and legal segregation may be gone, but the effects of past discrimination linger in seniority systems that preserve the results of a racially segmented job market, a black unemployment rate twice as high as that for whites, and pervasive housing segregation. People who claim that affirmative action stigmatizes its recipients are influenced by the notion that the "normal" American is white and that blacks who hold traditionally white jobs are interlopers. Whatever the faults of affirmative action, it has helped create a new black middle class, resting on professional and managerial positions within white society, that is especially vulnerable to economic and political winds. Eliminating affirmative action programs will do nothing to make society more meritocratic.

Without visible support. *National Review* 47:18+ Mr 20 '95

Affirmative action now seems to be without visible support, but it has shown that it can defy the usual gravitational principles. In politics. After the Republicans won both houses of Congress, the entire political establishment from the President on down agreed that affirmative action must be reformed. The issue, however, is not simply one of quotas but the idea that any preferences should be made on the basis of skin color or gender. Moreover, both public- and private-sector policies need to be reviewed and, if necessary, overturned; the concept of "disparate impact" discrimination, based on statistical representation, needs to be disavowed; preferences should not be allowed to survive in the form of providing benefits to the "economically disadvantaged"; and finally, Americans should be made aware of the national costs of affirmative action to the economy.

Quitting quotas. Rich Lowry. *National Review* 47:26+ Mr 20 '95

With the drafting of the California Civil Rights Initiative (CCRI), Republicans may not only halt but begin to reverse the post-1964 civil-rights revolution. Proposed by academics Glynn Custred and Thomas Wood, CCRI would prohibit the state from discriminating in its schools, contracting, and employment. Meanwhile, Clint Bolick, litigation director for the Institute for Justice, and a group of former Reagan and Bush administration officials are pushing for a much broader offensive—a federal initiative.

Tentatively titled the Civil Rights Act of 1995, it would prohibit the government from using race, national origin, sex, or any other such category as a "criterion in allocating opportunities in any manner whatsoever."

Son of 187: anti-affirmative action propositions. Peter Schrag. *The New Republic* 212:16+ Ja 30 '95

A California anti-affirmative action proposition has received renewed support since the Republicans gained control of the state assembly. As an amendment to the state constitution, the proposal would spike almost all affirmative action programs in state employment and higher education. It has already drawn the tacit support of Governor Pete Wilson. In view of the overwhelming white male support for Republicans in the 1994 elections, which carried a message of anger at anything hinting of preference for women and minorities, the initiative is likely to cause major difficulties for the Democrats. If they continue to back preferences, they will lose the white middle-class vote, but if they back the new initiative against affirmative action, they risk losing the support not only of minorities and women's groups but also of the liberal public employees' unions.

Class is in. Mickey Kaus. *The New Republic* 212:6 Mr 27 '95

Everyone, including President Clinton, seems to be searching for a compromise on affirmative action that would mitigate the existing system's poisonous side effects while still trying to compensate for the persistence of unequal opportunity. One possible compromise would be to replace race and gender with class as the basis for affirmative action. This widely applauded idea has obvious appeal in that it treats people as individuals and can be presented as an extension of meritocracy. However, the potential drawbacks of such a system suggest that class-based preferences should be sharply restricted. Class disadvantage would be at least as difficult to measure as race- or gender-based disadvantage, and class-based affirmative action would still reward people for nurturing group grievances.

Class, not race: an affirmative action that works. Richard D. Kahlenberg. *The New Republic* 212:21+ Ap 3 '95

President Clinton has the opportunity to turn the backlash against federal affirmative action programs into a political advantage without betraying basic Democratic principles. Clinton can accomplish this by incorporating the principle of race neutrality and the goal of aiding the disadvantaged into affirmative action preference programs themselves. In this scenario, preferences in education, entry-level employment, and public contracting would be based on class rather than race. If Clinton proposes this move, the media will charge him with lurching to the right. Yet the idea of class-based affirmative action, with its message of addressing class unfairness and its political potential for building cross-racial coalitions, should appeal to the left as well. The article discusses how class-based preference programs would work and refutes several objections to class-based preferences.

The color-blind court. Jeff Rosen. *The New Republic* 213:19-20+
Jl 31 '95

At least four Supreme Court justices—Clarence Thomas, Antonin Scalia,
William Rehnquist, and Anthony Kennedy—have firmly committed
themselves to the proposition that government can almost never classify
citizens on the basis of race. They think that through decisions made this
year they have finally exorcized the ghost of the Warren court, fulfilled
the goals of the conservative judicial revolution, and vindicated the ideal
of a color-blind Constitution for the first time since Reconstruction.
Among other things, they have paved the way for the judicial invalidation
of most forms of affirmative action by insisting that all racial preferences,
whether passed by Congress or the states, are presumptively unconstitutional unless narrowly designed as a remedy for past discrimination. The
writer discusses how the conservative judicial project has misrepresented
Reconstruction Republican opinion to validate its decisions in the race
cases of 1995.

The end of affirmative action. Joe Klein. *Newsweek* 125:36-7 F
13 '95

Affirmative action seems to be nearing its end in the United States. Over
the past twenty-five years, affirmative action has insinuated itself into every aspect of American public life and much of the private sector. Affirmative action has made it socially impossible to run any large institution
in a racially exclusionary manner, but it has also been divisive and funda-
mentally unfair. Affirmative action has sparked such controversy in part
because the policy has evolved almost entirely by executive order and
court fiat, without public debate. This will soon change, however. Upcoming Supreme Court cases and legislative initiatives in Washington and
in many states are likely to narrow the use of racial preference programs.
Blacks will probably react with anger and despair, while whites will probably respond with a disingenuous call for a "colorblind society." Possible
replacements for affirmative action are discussed.

What about women? Bob Cohn, Bill Turque, and Martha Brant.
Newsweek 125:22-5 Mr 27 '95

Proponents of affirmative action are struggling to shift the terms of the
turbulent national debate over the policy from race to gender. By most
measures, women have been the greatest beneficiaries of affirmative action. While African Americans have made only modest gains in the workplace in the last decade, women now hold more than 40 percent of all
corporate middle-management jobs, and businesses owned by women
have grown by more than 57 percent since 1982. Some Clinton aides
seem to think that playing the gender card can help save affirmative action. Still, the President faces a course full of political obstacles. To keep
his party's liberal base intact, he must blunt the Republican assault on affirmative action. To win back the middle-class men he needs for reelec-

tion, however, he'll have to show that he is not just a defender of the status quo.

The myth of meritocracy. Ellis Cose. *Newsweek* 125:34 Ap 3 '95

Critics of affirmative action contend that its elimination will put society on a course toward a colorblind, gender-neutral paradise in which personal achievement is honored and favoritism is defunct. However, these critics have not explained how abolishing affirmative action can lead to a meritocracy when other forms of favoritism continue to thrive. They have also not shown any real enthusiasm for attacking preferential treatment in all its guises, increasing enforcement of anti-discrimination laws, or devoting more resources to inner-city schools. In general, they are not proposing anything that might eventually move the U.S. closer to the meritocracy they profess to desire. Instead, they are merely turning affirmative action into a scapegoat.

Back to basic. Joe Klein. *Newsweek* 125:35 Ap 24 '95

President Clinton should use the example of the U.S. military to show how affirmative action can benefit people. One reason why the military is the main institution that has most successfully practiced affirmative action is its adherence to inclusion, not preferences. This, after all, was what the original spirit of affirmative action intended. The military's implicit contract with enlistees holds that if they meet military standards and play by the military's rules, one's ability to advance will be solely determined by merit. It helps that rank is more important than race in the military, but the military has also taken positive steps to ensure that discrimination isn't tolerated. The only way Clinton can end racial preference programs is to propose an alternative, and an aggressive program of inclusion targeting poor teens may be the most plausible.

Backlash against affirmative action troubles advocates. Steven A. Holmes. *New York Times* B9 F 7 '95

Supporters of affirmative-action programs find chilling the prospect of affirmative action being debated in a Republican-dominated Congress with a Presidential election on the horizon. Several Republicans are eager to approve anti-affirmative-action measures and to dare the President to veto them, confident that he will lose support among white men if he does.

Black executives forming group to defend minority programs. Steven A. Holmes. *New York Times* A16 My 11 '95

Black Enterprise Magazine publisher Earl G. Graves and other black business executives announced today that they are forming a political action committee called Mobilization for Economic Opportunity and hiring a lobbyist to fight efforts to eliminate affirmative action programs. The executives' effort comes at a time when affirmative action programs—

especially those that set aside a percentage of government contracts for minority-owned companies—are under increasing attack, mainly by Republicans.

Seeds of racial explosion. Timur Kuran. *Society* 30:55–67 S/O '93

The quiet resignation of American whites to affirmative action programs for blacks has had several socially significant consequences. Whites fear being accused of racism if they speak their true thoughts about affirmative action, but their restraint has made race relations seem more harmonious than they actually are, has concealed the potential for a white backlash, has helped block the emergence of more popular responses to racial disparity, and has discouraged intellectuals from speaking openly and frankly on matters pertaining to race. The writer discusses the implications of hidden white resentment for American politics, the failure of affirmative action to help the black underclass, the regulation of race-related intellectual discourse, the potential for open racial confrontations between blacks and whites, and the emergence of dissenters who are beginning to restore freedom of speech on racial matters.

A new push for blind justice. Richard Lacayo. *Time* 145:39–40 F 20 '95

Misgivings about affirmative action are reaching a critical mass. The new Republican majority in Congress is preparing to position Democrats as die-hard defenders of preferential treatment for minorities. A 1994 *Times Mirror* poll reveals that a majority of whites agree that society has gone too far in pushing equal rights in this country. Several cases have been filed in federal courts by angry whites challenging race-based preferences, and Californians are expected to vote on a ballot initiative next year that would prohibit preferences for women and minorities in state programs. A recent *Time*/CNN poll of eight hundred adults shows that 77 percent think affirmative action discriminates against whites. Even among black respondents, 66 percent answered the same way. Skeptical judges may trim affirmative action at the federal level and in the Supreme Court.

Turning back the clock. Jeffrey H. Birnbaum. *Time* 145:36–7 Mr 20 '95

Affirmative-action programs appear to be on the chopping block in Washington. The Republicans are not debating whether affirmative action will be razed but only how quickly the dismantling will occur. Many Democrats accept the inevitable; President Clinton is reviewing all 160 affirmative-action programs and is expected to recommend that some of them be cut. Affirmative action will not die without a fight, however, as groups representing blacks, Hispanics, and women prepare to combine their lobby forces to preserve as many programs as possible.

Does affirmative action have a future? Robert J. Bresler. *USA Today* 123:7 S '94

The future of affirmative action in America is uncertain. Supporters of affirmative action programs must stand on a firm political base to be effective, yet political support is currently fragile. Meanwhile, the departure from the Supreme Court of liberal justices William Brennan, Thurgood Marshall, and Harry Blackmun over the last few years is a reminder that affirmative action rests on shifting judicial grounds. Controversial social change cannot rest upon the courts, however, and even the most sympathetic judicial decisions are no substitute for public support. Affirmative action can survive in its present form if the concept is reconstructed to draw upon two central ideas of the civil rights movement: that justice for people should be based upon their status as individuals, not members of groups, and that a commitment must be made to a truly integrated society.

Endgame for affirmative action. John Leo. *U.S. News & World Report* 118:18 Mr 13 '95

Affirmative action has never had much support among the American electorate. Between 80 and 90 percent of whites and a majority of non-whites, according to surveys, oppose affirmative action when any hint of racial preference is included in pollsters' questions. Title VII, Section 703 of the 1964 Civil Rights Act plainly bans preferences by race, gender, ethnicity, and religion in business and government. Unfortunately, the act was converted by bureaucrats and judges into a system of proportional representation by race. Dissent against affirmative action is portrayed by the left as a temper tantrum of whiny, white males. Rather, it is a nationwide revulsion for the politics of group rights, quotas, and preferences that lie at the heart of the policy.

Back to the politicians. Ted Gest. *U.S. News & World Report* 118:38-9 Je 26 '95

A recent Supreme Court ruling on reserving federal contracts for minorities is expected to fuel the battle over affirmative action. In the case of *Adarand Constructors v. Pena*, the Court ruled 5-4 that the U.S. Transportation Department had unfairly favored a Hispanic contractor over the white-owned Adarand firm when awarding a Colorado guardrail contract. Rather than settling the issue of so-called federal set asides, however, the decision promises to ignite further political wrangling and litigation. Still, the Court delivered the overarching message in its decision that racial preferences are rarely acceptable. Civil rights advocates view this trend as ominous, while Republicans laud the ruling as a mandate for more cuts in affirmative action.